CAPS, VAMPS, AND MITTENS
FROM THE ISLAND OF NEWFOUNDLAND

SALTWATER
Classics

BOULDER
BOOKS

CHRISTINE LEGROW & SHIRLEY A. SCOTT

Library and Archives Canada Cataloguing in Publication

Title: Saltwater classics from the island of Newfoundland : more than 25 caps, vamps, and mittens to
   knit / Christine LeGrow and Shirley A. Scott.
Other titles: More than twenty-five caps, vamps and mittens to knit
Names: LeGrow, Christine, 1953- author. | Scott, Shirley A., 1947- author.
Identifiers: Canadiana 20190130865 | ISBN 9781989417010 (softcover)
Subjects: LCSH: Knitting—Newfoundland and Labrador—Patterns. | LCSH: Knitwear—Newfoundland and
   Labrador. | LCSH: Knitting—Newfoundland and Labrador—History.
Classification: LCC TT819.C32 N49 2019 | DDC 746.43/20432—dc23

10 9 8 7 6 5 4 3 2 1

We acknowledge the financial support of the Government of Newfoundland and Labrador through the Department of Tourism, Culture, Industry and Innovation.

We acknowledge the financial support for our publishing program by the Government of Canada and the Department of Canadian Heritage through the Canada Book Fund.

To those who lived here always

To those who had to leave

To those who came from away

CONTENTS

FOREWORD

Tradition is a curious thing.

It comes from the past, but it lives in the present, carrying ideas into the future. It is shared knowledge passed down from hand to hand and heart to heart. The oral transmission of ideas across generations is at the centre of tradition, and what keeps things such as knitting skills and techniques alive. But that very informality in the way that skills are passed along is potentially also the thin spot where tradition is likely to unravel. If one generation fails to pass their know-how on to the next, what happens to centuries worth of accumulated expertise?

In the old folktales of Newfoundland and Labrador, the hero or heroine often sets off on a journey not really knowing much at all. Along the way it is not uncommon for them to be aided by a wise woman who provides the enchanted object or prudent counsel they need to complete their quest. Without that person's knowledge and assistance, nothing would ever get done in fairy tales.

So it is with tradition, and over the past decade Christine LeGrow and Shirley Anne Scott have emerged as fairy godmothers in the local knitting scene. They magically seem to be everywhere, sharing their knowledge, teaching skills, preparing patterns, publishing, giving sage advice on radio phone-in shows, and darning the odd sock. They are enthusiastic supporters of our culture, always working to keep our textile traditions alive, current, and colourful.

In their previous volume in this series, *Saltwater Mittens*, they expertly and painstakingly recreated more than 20 heritage patterns. Recognizing that heritage sometimes needs a little push, they have continued their work to safeguard this beloved Newfoundland and Labrador art form, and in this volume expand upon their previous efforts, adding further designs for caps, vamps, and mittens. If you don't have a Nan to help you on your adventure, Christine and Shirley have you covered, including tips your grandmother would have been sure to pass along.

They aren't bad storytellers themselves either, and this book is proof of that. These patterns speak to the people, history, landscape, and music of this place. You'll meet some old familiar faces, from Harry Hibbs to Émile Benoît. You might lose your heart to the Star of Logy Bay, and maybe come face to face with one of the Mockbeggar spooks or the spirit of a long-vanished Norseman. Watch out for that thin ice on Tickle Cove Pond as you journey along.

Enjoy this book, and happy knitting. Remember that you are now part of this tradition. Pass along what you know, and keep this story alive for future generations.

Dale Gilbert Jarvis, Folklorist,
Clarke's Beach, Newfoundland.

INTRODUCTION

Noggin Cove, single band.

It is once again our pleasure to tell through knitting a little of the story of life in Newfoundland.

Writing our first book, *Saltwater Mittens*, was like casting our bread upon the waters and having it come back with butter and molasses on it. That book spoke to experienced knitters, career knitters, returning knitters, and beginning knitters. For a short while we foolishly believed we had said all there was to say, but, as time went by, we realized there were still many stories to tell. Ideas began to sprout and bloom in our minds like hyacinths in winter. New designs for classic Newfoundland garments foamed off the needles. We dusted off our big computers and got back to work. The projects in *Saltwater Classics* touch on our history and geography, our weather and music, and our strong love of home and family.

You leave a bit of Canada behind when you wash ashore here. After all, where else do vamps, a type of footwear, still form part of a winter wardrobe? Our place names ring with expression. Caps with names like Noggin Cove and Tickle Cove come with smiles from home in them. Vamps from Little Heart's Ease offer a sense of security and protection. To bless with food, clothing, and, above all, with love is the Newfoundland way. To provide good warm garments for confronting harsh, ungovernable elements and shocking hardships is the work of the saltwater knitter.

Diamond vamps.

Something was not quite right but it didn't click until I saw Nan rocking in the window. It meant there was a hard blow coming and Nan would be spending the day in her chair. We didn't get many summer storms so it was a surprise to see my Nan quivering like a bowl of crabapple jelly. The weather looked fine to me, hardly anything except a gentle breeze from the east. I made the tea and brought Nan a mug and a biscuit. She ate and drank without a word. She didn't take her eyes off the harbour.

—Mary C. Sheppard, *Seven for a Secret*

We need such blessings. We struggle against great forces. Our culture has been shaken by diaspora and resettlement. People and wealth drain away from Newfoundland like blood from a wound. Our Hello Goodbye Mitten is a tribute to all the comings and goings throughout the history of this place. The Helmet, inspired by life at L'Anse aux Meadows, celebrates the Viking exploration of Newfoundland. Plaisance Gloves for Ladies commemorate the rich, historic Basque and French fisheries in the Placentia Bay area. Mockbeggar Mitts for Youngsters speak of the experience of early settlers at the Mockbeggar Plantation in Bonavista. Past and present mingle here in an extraordinary way.

Plaisance gloves.

There are those among us who aspire to California dress of course, but for much of the year the snow is just too deep, the wind too boisterous, the fog too thick, and the rain too sideways to sustain tropical illusions. Our classic designs for head, hands, and feet are pure, enduring, Newfoundland all-season style. Consider each project a personal voyage into a time and place. You'll be as happy as a gull with a herring. We promise you.

Helmet.

Noggin Cove Cap with Streely Maid Wrister.

There is one sure thing that can be said about Newfoundland: it is unforgettable. Anyone born there remains a Newfoundlander, first and foremost.

It's said that Newfoundlanders are always easy to spot in Heaven. They're the ones who keep nagging God to let them go back home. Who could blame those disconnected spirits for wanting to go back home? Where else will they find a stranger who feels like family? Where else will they find a stranger who often turns out to be family?

—SHIRLEY MURPHY, *ALLAN SQUARE: A ST. JOHN'S MEMOIR*

Boots, the intrepid cat.

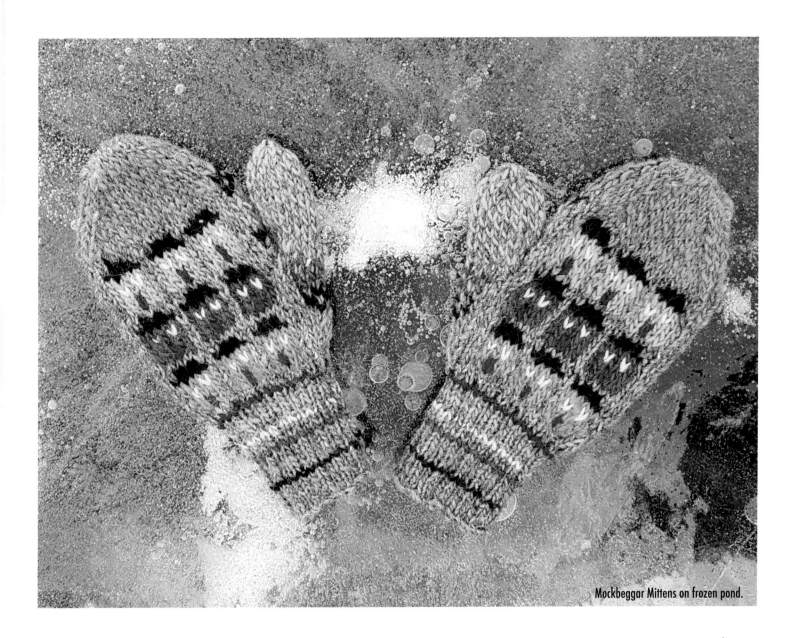

Mockbeggar Mittens on frozen pond.

Mauzy Day knits.

COLOURS, TEXTURES, AND YARNS

Why do so many artists live in Newfoundland? The artistic impulse is enduring and omnipresent among people, but why did it flourish so in Newfoundland, a place of hard toil? It seems inexplicable, but we continue to admire the care that Newfoundlanders of days gone by lavished on making everything from socks to chairs, to wooden boats, to a loaf of bread. On cooking, music making, dancing, and singing. On words and on stitches.

She's bordered by inlets,
tickles and sounds,

Reaches, by coves and by bays,

She soothes your vision as you
sail 'round her shores

With a mixture of greens,
browns and grays.

—BUDDY WASISNAME AND THE OTHER FELLERS, "SONG FOR NEWFOUNDLAND"

Emotions colour our world, and our world colours our emotions. Duckish, the word used to describe twilight in Newfoundland, is as cool and subdued as the dying day. Soft colours have particular appeal here. We are *connoisseurs* of blue, green, grey, and brown, the colours of the rocks, trees, fog, and water we see for much of the year. They bring peace. Gentle pastel combinations like grey and white, common in both vintage and modern knitting, have been popular here for centuries. Our Fog Eats Snow colourway is named after a well-known spring weather phenomenon and Mauzy Day is a combination of the many shades of blue and grey that nature can muster. Brightly painted houses around our shores continue to bring joy also. Witless Bay celebrates the comforting seaside

MAUZY

Damp and warm, muggy, close, foggy. Sometimes with a very light rain or condensation on objects and a cool, gentle wind off the sea.

"Breeze comin' from duh suddard," the skipper said. "Always blows up mauzy weather." And the fog did indeed roll over the deep as the warm south wind hit the chill air of the bank.
—DICTIONARY OF NEWFOUNDLAND ENGLISH

Left: Witless Bay with blue.
Below: Witless Bay home.

home of dear friends. Other bright combinations in this book spring from the simple joy of knitting with beautiful yarn.

Good weather is so elusive that we have not developed the same richness of vocabulary to describe it. Smoky skies and stormy seas speak to us often. All Newfoundlanders are passionate about forecasting the weather. We study it constantly, watching especially for signs of mayhem. There is so much sky to look at that it is not at all surprising so many of our knitted colourways are rooted in such an observation. First Light suggests clear early morning skies, dark hills silhouetted against the blue light. Will it be a fine, large day? Winter Dawn captures frosty clouds of creamy pastel on a polar pale background.

Uncle John had first gone to sea at the age of eight with his father, jigging fish from a dory. He was a late starter. Uncle Jim had begun his career at seven as cabin boy aboard his grandfather's small schooner fishing down the Labrador. Salt water was almost their blood. As Howard said of them, "They be as well pickled as the finest Madeira."

—FARLEY MOWAT, *BAY OF SPIRITS*

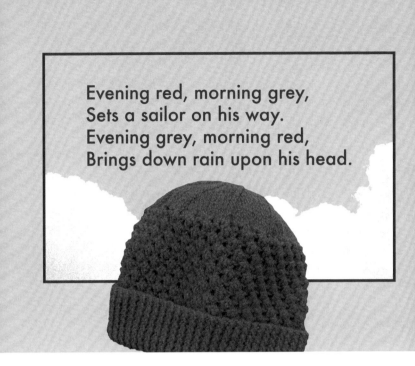

Evening red, morning grey,
Sets a sailor on his way.
Evening grey, morning red,
Brings down rain upon his head.

Red sky at morning,
Sailors take warning.
Red sky at night,
Sailors' delight.

Vivid skies may also carry a warning of weather later in the day. As newcomers to Newfoundland soon discover, "weather" almost always means bad weather. Sailors Take Warning, by AnnMarie MacCrae, paints an intense morning sky that thrills and threatens at the same time. We know these treacherous skies well. The sensitive and sophisticated shadings of Milly Brown's Blue Moon suggest those mystical night skies that crackle with energy at certain points in the lunar cycle when plants quicken their growth, fish spawn, and people are breathless with beauty.

Tickle Cove arch.

Boreal chickadee.

We live in a world of rich textures too. The scrubby junipers, berry bushes, and shrubs of the barrens, the tuckamores and rocky outcrops, a seascape here, boreal forest there, all these have also inspired our designs. The dramatic arch of Tickle Cove is subtly evoked in seed stitch in the Tickle Cove Cap. The honeycombs and cables of the Brigus Boot Sock suggest ropes that hoisted sails and moored ships on luscious summer days. You'll imagine the many plump, juicy wild berries that grow here, free for the taking, in the bumpy texture of the Trinity Cap. Choose your colour—partridgeberry, cranberry, raspberry, blueberry, or chuckly pear. If only we could convey the scent of plants and fresh sea air!

Perhaps Newfoundlanders have more opportunity than others to soak up the beauty that surrounds us and to give it back in the form of art. It is our particular pleasure to share the beauty around us through knitting. Saltwater knitters live for choosing colours. We love them all, the bold ones, the soothing ones, and those as vibrant as Mary Pratt jellies.

SOME FAVOURITE COLOURWAYS

Although all our samples were knit with the specific brands of yarn described here, we have used generic names for these colours. Because many of our gifted friends and fellow knitters have developed colour stories of startling originality, we are pleased to feature some of them in this book.

Nautical Blood.

Blue Moon, *by Milly Brown.* Royal Blue. Sage. Forest Brown. Lilac.

Boreal. Green. Grey. Tan. Brown. White.

Candy Cane. Red. Bright White.

Duckish. Midnight Blue. Lilac. Mauve.

First Light. Midnight Blue. Misty Blue.

Fog Eats Snow. Mauve. Bright White.

Lupins. Purple. White. Mauve. Pink.

Mauzy Day. Misty Blue. Dusty Blue. Light Grey. Medium Grey. Dark Grey.

Nautical Blood, *by Mary Dawn Greenwood.* Natural White. Navy Blue. Red. Turquoise.

Rock 'n' Roll. Yellow. Light Green. Scarlet. Pink. Mauve.

Rosa Rugosa, *by Milly Brown.* Red. Sage. Pink. Bright White.

Sailors Take Warning, *by AnnMarie MacCrae.* Pink. Pale Blue. Yellow.

Terra Nova. Dark Green. Forest Brown. Yellow.

Wassail. Dark Green. Scarlet.

Winter Dawn. Natural White. Mauve. Pink. Lilac.

Witless Bay. Yellow. Red. Dark Green. Royal Blue (optional).

Blue Moon.

Candy Cane.

Sailors Take Warning.

Rock 'n' Roll.

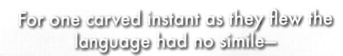

For one carved instant as they flew the
language had no simile—

Silver, crystal, ivory were tarnished.
Etched upon the horizon blue ...

—E.J. PRATT, "SEA GULLS"

Lupins.

Rosa Rugosa.

YARNS

Most of our garments are made from woollen spun yarns in yarn weight Group 3 (light worsted) and Group 4 (medium worsted). A few use sport weight yarn from Group 2 (fine). All samples in this book were knit with yarns from the Briggs and Little Woolen Mill in Harvey Station, New Brunswick, Canada. Yarn quantities specified in the patterns are rounded upward.

When it comes to choosing knitting yarns today, our cup runneth over. Beautiful luxury yarns make soft, elegant vamps, mittens, and caps, but use only sturdy, pure wool if you want your Saltwater Classics to stand the test of time and hard wear. Yarn substitution is a sport everyone excels at, because, no matter where we live, so little of what we see advertised is available locally. The following describes the yarn used in the samples. We hope it will make choosing an equivalent easier.

Briggs and Little Regal. 2-ply 100% wool. Yarn Group 3 (light worsted weight). 20 stitches = 10 cm on 4.50 mm needles. Put up: 4-ounce skeins. 272 yards per skein.

1 skein = 272 yards = approximately 250 metres
½ skein = 135 yards = approximately 125 metres

Briggs and Little Heritage. 2-ply 100% wool. Yarn Group 4 (medium worsted weight). 17 stitches = 10 cm on 5.00 mm needles. Put up: 4-ounce skeins. 215 yards per skein.

1 skein = 215 yards = approximately 200 metres
½ skein = 107 yards = approximately 100 metres

Briggs and Little Sport. 1-ply 100% wool. Yarn Group 2 (fine weight). 24 stitches = 10 cm on 3.00 mm needles. Put up: 4-ounce skeins. 430 yards per skein.

1 skein = 430 yards = approximately 375 metres
½ skein = 215 yards = approximately 195 metres

Vive La Rose Trigger Mitt (left),
Wesleyville Trigger Mitt.

TERMS AND ABBREVIATIONS

CARRYING YARNS. Always carry the dark yarn on the left and the light yarn on the right to prevent streaks in the colour work. This is essential in double ball knitting. Some people also express this as carrying the light yarn over and the dark yarn under, without crossing them.

DOUBLE BALL KNITTING, DOUBLE KNITTING, DOUBLE KNIT. These are alternative names used in Newfoundland for fairisle or stranded colourwork. Newfoundland double knitting should not be confused with tubular double knitting.

DOUBLE POINTED NEEDLES. Straight needles with points at both ends, usually used in small circumference circular knitting. Our instructions are written for sets of 4 needles, three to hold the stitches and one working needle. More may be used.

GRAFTING. A common method of seamlessly closing the toe of a sock or vamp. The raw loops of the unfinished edges are joined by stitches made with a sewing needle. They imitate a row of knitted stitches perfectly. Brigus Boot Socks and Family Vamps, for example, provide excellent instructions.

JOGLESS STRIPES. They have no "stair step" at the point where a new colour is joined at the beginning of a round. Use them on the wrists of mittens for a professional touch. To make stripes jogless, work the first round of the new colour in the required stitch. On the second round of the new colour, slip the first stitch of the round to the right needle purlwise without working it, then continue in pattern to the end of the round. This shifts the beginning of the round one stitch to the left. When ribbing is complete, reinstating the original beginning of the round is optional. Jogless stripes are often combined with tidy stripes. Detailed instructions for this technique appear on the wrist of the Plaisance Gloves.

MAKE 1 RIGHT (M1R). MAKE 1 LEFT (M1L). These paired increases are used in the thumb gusset of a Newfoundland mitten and are made with the colour indicated on the gusset chart. We favour the "half-hitch make 1" method of increasing for some of our projects. Other methods may also be used.

PICKET-FENCE SHAPING. A picket-fence shaping comes to a point at the top of a toe or mitten. To create a picket-fence top, work decreases at four points in salt and pepper pattern on *every* round until too few stitches remain to work a full repeat. Break yarns, thread one yarn through the remaining loops, draw tight, and secure.

Streely Maid Classic Mitten with picket-fence top.

ROUND TOP SHAPING. To create a round top on a mitten, two S&P decrease rounds are followed by a round with no decreases, ending shaping with a no decrease round. Trigger mitts usually have a round top. Classic mittens may have either round or picket-fence hand shapings. Some knitters mix both styles. Round tops are usually cast off with the 3-needle bind off.

SEGMENT MARKERS. Stitch markers, usually rings, that separate the sections of a circular garment. They may be a different colour from the marker at the beginning of the round. Loops of yarn also work well.

S&P. SALT AND PEPPER PATTERN. This distinctive pattern is a mainstay in Newfoundland knitting, filling areas such as thumbs, trigger fingers, palms of hands, mitten tops, and other areas requiring shaping. This famous pattern is very warm, versatile, and gives Newfoundland mittens their character. When worked on an odd number of stitches, it has a seamless appearance and the beginning of a new round is invisible. Mittens, thumbs, and fingers may be lengthened by adding rounds of S&P as needed before shaping. Decreasing in S&P requires close attention to instructions.

SKP. SLIP, KNIT, PASS. Slip one stitch as if to knit. Knit 1 stitch. Pass slipped stitch over.

SSK. SLIP, SLIP, KNIT. A left-leaning decrease used to shape knitted pieces. It has a neater appearance than SKP, which does the same job. Also used effectively to finish the tops of fingers and thumbs. To work SSK, slip 2 stitches knitwise, one at a time. Insert left needle through the front of these two stitches from left to right and knit them together through the back of the loop with the required colour. SSK is one of two decreases used to shape the top of mittens and vamps. The corresponding decrease which leans to the right is K2tog.

TBL. Through the back of the loop.

THUMB AND FINGER DECREASES. Thumb, trigger finger, and glove fingertips require two decrease rounds to complete in S&P pattern.

THUMB GUSSET INCREASES. Thumb gussets are an important feature of Newfoundland mittens. Gusset increases are made in S&P inside an outline stitch and may be dark or light, as the chart indicates. The outline stitch stays the same colour throughout, but the increases vary. Any good increase method will work, but we favour the backward loop (half-hitch) method. Professional-looking gusset increases also lean to the right and left as indicated on the chart. For the neatest work use M1R and M1L increases in the colour indicated.

TIDY STRIPES. Tidy stripes are not traditional but they give a handsome finished appearance to ribbing. We have coined the name but the technique is an old one. The colour of one tidy stripe does not bleed into the colour of an adjacent stripe.

A tidy stripe must be at least two rows deep. To make stripes in ribbing tidy work the first round of each new colour in plain knitting. Resume ribbing on the second round of the new colour. Tidy stripes may be combined with jogless stripes. Detailed instructions are offered in Plaisance Gloves.

3-NEEDLE BIND OFF. A signature technique used to finish a round top mitten smoothly. It is worked on the wrong side, with the mitten turned inside out. It is used here in place of two-colour grafting, a much more difficult technique not common in Newfoundland. Trigger mitts are usually finished with the 3-needle bind off. Nan at Your Side offers some helpful suggestions.

TURN. A method of making short rows used most often when turning the heels of socks and vamps. When knitting with the right side of the work facing, for example, "turn" means reversing the work so that the wrong side is facing before making the next stitch on the wrong side.

"See that!" Yark gripped Quoyle's wrist, drew his arm out to follow his own, pointing northeast into the bay. Out on the darkling water a ball of blue fire glimmered. The lighthouse flash cut across the bay, revealed nothing, and in the stunned darkness behind it the strange glow rolled and faded.

"That's a weather light. Seen them many times. Bad weather coming."

—E. ANNIE PROULX, *THE SHIPPING NEWS*

Noggin Cove.

DEGREES OF DIFFICULTY

Not much about traditional Newfoundland knitting is simple. We wish we could promise otherwise. We continue to marvel at the complexity of vintage garments knit without written instructions. In *Saltwater Classics* because we seek to initiate readers gently into the mysteries of Newfoundland knitting, our patterns are graded by difficulty.

Our easiest designs, such as the Landfall Watch Cap and Family Vamps, can be knit when hove off on the sofa, being companionable and pretending to watch the hockey game. You will be flushed with knitting success.

After the scales have fallen from your eyes, get ready for something a bit more tangly. Most classic Newfoundland knitting falls into this category and it takes a bit of learning and practice to be good at it. As we say here, you'll be as busy as a bayman with two wood stoves. But with Nan at Your Side tips placed just where you need them, what could possibly go wrong?

As to the effect on your own heart of knitting the complex Diamond Vamps from Little Heart's Ease, we hesitate to speculate. Instead, we offer the consolation of philosophy.

He was the best kind starting off. Maybe he was hove off on the couch too much, took a bit too much time with the grooming, had to look awfully sleek when he went out. But you'd put up with that.

—CARMELITA MCGRATH, "OLD CROOKED FELLOW"

✳ EASY DOES IT

Shag-ups build character. Once you learn to sing the song it's easy peasy. The journey is more important than the arrival. Walk before you run. *Namaste.*

✳✳ TANGLY

Practice by patting your head and rubbing your belly at the same time. Ride the tide. There's no gain without pain. Never give up the ship! *Namaste.*

✳✳✳ OVER THE WHARF

Oh, me nerves! We never promised you a rose garden. Would a man running for his life notice your mistakes? *Namaste.*

Nan
AT YOUR
Side

All *Saltwater Classics* patterns are written in detail. We favour simple, well-known methods of construction that require little explanation. Newfoundland knitters of times past had no written patterns, yet their mittens, caps, and vamps were practical works of art. Once you learn the essential way of making them, it becomes easy. That's a promise.

"Dad, Beety is showing me how to knit. I am knitting a Christmas present for you. It's very hard."

"Good lord," said Quoyle, astonished. "And you're only four years old."

"It's a kind of a trick, Dad, because it's just a long, long, fat string and it turns into a scarf."

—E. ANNIE PROULX, *THE SHIPPING NEWS*

Taking care of our readers is of great importance to us but it can be difficult to communicate all the clever tricks learned by trial and error over the years in formal knitting patterns. If only Nan were here to help!

Relax and breathe deeply. Nan has your back. Her tips for neater knitting are the next best thing. Study them carefully. When a tip pertains specifically to a single pattern, Nan and her helping hand will be exactly where you need her, beside the pattern in question. Watch for Nan's advice. More general tips are offered below.

Is it Nan's way or the highway? Nan would go to the wall to defend some of her tips. Some of them may indeed be controversial, but the world of knitting is wide and its wisdom deep. Keep an open mind.

BRIDGING GAPS. When casting on to close the gap of a thumb gusset or trigger finger, do not try to pull the yarn too tightly. It will only look loose and untidy until a round or two of stitches is worked above it. Then it becomes firm and neat. It's a miracle.

WEAVING IN YARN FLOATS NAN'S WAY. In colour patterns such as Streely Maid and Noggin Cove, where there are more than three adjacent stitches of one colour, long floats of background colour develop behind the pattern colour. These must be caught (or *woven in*) to keep the public surface of the knitted piece smooth and even. Nan has some strong ideas about this. Here they are.

• Weave in floating yarns as seldom as possible, not as often as possible.

• Make no more than three stitches of a single colour without catching the floating yarn of the other colour. Fewer than three is fine, but more troublesome.

• If a diamond pattern has a single contrasting centre stitch,

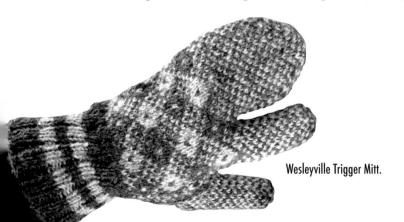

Wesleyville Trigger Mitt.

as in the Wesleyville Trigger Mitts, the universe is unfolding as it should and life will be easy. Simply catch the float when making the stitch directly above or below this centre stitch.

• Weave a dark float into a dark stitch and a light float into a light stitch. Never weave a dark float into a light stitch unless you have no choice. It will be hard to hide from friends who hold your work up to their razor-sharp eyes.

• Never weave a float into a stitch that caught a float in the previous row. Space them out.

• Weaving a float into the first or last stitch on a double pointed needle helps prevent ladders forming between the needles—if that's the sort of thing that bothers you.

CUSTOM FIT FOR TRIGGER MITTS. To get the very best custom fit, first complete the thumb, then the trigger finger, then the hand shaping. This is contrary to many instructions. They are not often written this way, because it is slower and

> Aunt Sue was up cleaning the old Waterloo before she lit the fire and the stove would get too hot ... She had an old wool sock hauled over her hand for the final touch to the stove. I couldn't see how she could make it shine more than it already did, but she gave it a brisk once-over, then neatly folded the sock, put it in the blackening box, and stored it under the stairs.
>
> —C. MILLY JOHNSON, "MAURA FALTON"

involves much putting stitches on holders and taking them off again. But it does guarantee the best fit, and Nan swears by it. Your mitt will fit you like a slap in the face, as we sometimes say in Newfoundland. And remember, the lucky person who will wear the mitts ought to be nearby to try them on at every step. If not, somebody may end up crying.

DARN THOSE VAMPS! Darning vamps and socks before they get holes in them is so sensible Nan wonders why everyone doesn't do it. As all old-timers know, a stitch in time saves nine. A stitch made before time might save even more. When your new vamp or sock is finished, turn it inside out. Use the ends waiting to be darned in or cut several lengths of yarn, then darn in a zigzag across the heel, toe, and any area that needs reinforcing. Pre-darned socks last much longer.

DARNING ENDS IN DOUBLE BALL KNITTING. Remember to darn into the back of an actual stitch, not a yarn float. Three or four darning stitches is enough to secure the ends. Do not trim too closely. When using 1-ply yarn, use a sharp needle and split the strand for extra security.

FINISHING. Double ball knitting often looks lumpy when it comes off the needles, even when done by experts like Nan and her crowd. A light pressing under a damp cloth or with a steam iron makes all the difference. Never press ribbing.

LENGTHENING OR SHORTENING. When changing the number of rounds from what is printed in the pattern, be sure to write the new number down. For mittens and vamps make both hands or feet the same! People will thank you for it.

NEATER RIBBING. When making a purl stitch after a knit stitch, the yarn path is longer than when following one knit stitch with another knit stitch. Ribbing may therefore look untidy. Machines and robots never have this problem; humble hand knitters may. To shorten the yarn path, insert the needle into the purl stitch normally, then wrap the yarn clockwise instead of counter clockwise to make the stitch. The stitch that results will be neater but twisted. Do not panic. Work into the back of it on the following row to restore it.

SALT AND PEPPER (S&P). DECREASING. It's tangly. Remember the decrease pattern this way. Next stitch, then same stitch. N comes before S in the alphabet. What could be easier?

PICKING UP STITCHES IN SALT AND PEPPER. HOLES. After so many struggles with the needles, Nan certainly knows that *knit happens.* Holes sometimes appear when picking up stitches. In salt and pepper pattern you can't simply pick up extra stitches where needed and get rid of them on the next round as you can with solid colours. When you join colours, always leave a long tail. It comes in handy. A little clever needlework with this tail will close holes on the wrong side. Even the best knitters in Newfoundland use this dodge. But they don't always talk about it.

3-NEEDLE BIND OFF. TURNING MITTENS INSIDE OUT. The easiest way to turn a mitten inside out for the bind off is to put stitches of the front and stitches of the palm each on a thin, short circular needle before turning. The flexibility of the needles makes turning inside out without dropping stitches easier. And when the mitten is safely turned, without any stitches escaping, you can bind off from these same holding needles. Nan's way does require some investment in needles, of course.

If you don't have thin, short circulars, lengths of string or smooth yarn are the next best. They are flexible for turning, but stitches must then be transferred to holding needles to bind off. Nan doesn't like to use rigid stitch holders shaped like safety pins because they are not flexible and sometimes open halfway through the turning operation. And then there will be tears before bedtime.

TOPPING OFF THUMBS AND FINGERS. Cut a 3-inch tail of the yarn colour used in the last stitch worked. Cut the remaining colour the usual length and poke its end into the tube of the thumb or finger for later darning. In Nan's opinion, ends left to dangle on the right side of the work can be hard to hide later. Thread the 3-inch tail into each of the remaining loops knitwise, then tighten. Poke it into the centre of the stitch of the opposite colour directly below it. This hides the finish very well.

TURNING A MITTEN INTO A WRISTER. If you lose the will to live halfway through a pattern, it's easy to turn saltwater mittens into wristers. Teenagers love them. Work the wrist, thumb gusset, and hand as for a regular mitten to the end of the pattern section of the hand. Choose a trim colour and break any unwanted hand colours. Knit one round with the trim colour, decreasing 6–8 stitches evenly spaced in the round. Work 2 rounds more in rib. Cast off in ribbing. **Thumb.** Put the stitches of the thumb gusset on two double pointed needles. Knit these stitches with the trim colour, then pick up and knit a few stitches at the base of the thumb. Join in a circle and work two rounds of ribbing. Cast off in rib. Detailed instructions are provided in the Streely Maid pattern.

Wrister on caribou moss.

WHAT MAKES A NEWFOUNDLAND MITTEN?

Although they have relatives in the gloves and mittens of Britain, Scandinavia, the Baltic, New England, and the Maritime provinces of Canada, Newfoundland mittens are special in the world of knitting. In the old days many knitters here had little access to manufactured yarn and patterns. Consequently, although their skill was great, they were unable to work from the abbreviations and codes of printed patterns. Their way of constructing mittens was passed down from generation to generation, developing a few signature features. It is these that give our mittens their distinctiveness. Here are some ways of recognizing a Newfoundland mitten.

RIBBED, STRIPED WRIST. Many types of ribbing are used, including twisted rib. (K2, P1) has always been a favourite. One round of dark ribbing followed by one round of contrasting ribbing is traditional and is still popular, but creating a new stripe sequence is one of the greatest pleasures of making Newfoundland mittens today. Our designs include a variety for your appreciation.

THUMB GUSSET. A thumb gusset is the triangle of stitches worked at the base of the thumb to allow freedom of movement. It is usual to highlight the thumb gusset with a decorative line of light or dark stitches at each side of the triangle. Thumb gussets in Newfoundland are usually worked in Salt and Pepper.

SALT AND PEPPER (S&P) PATTERN. Extensive use of this versatile pattern on the palm, the thumb, and the top of the mitten is a Newfoundland trademark. S&P consists of alternating dark and light stitches. On the following round a light stitch is made over a dark and a dark over a light. A simple looking binary system, it has a surprising number of quirks a knitter must master. Using S&P at strategic places makes it easy to create a custom fit, a great common-sense feature.

OPTIONAL "TRIGGER FINGER." This feature is not exclusive to Newfoundland but is so iconic that most people think it originated here. "Trigger finger" is a term of art. This finger is highly useful in a place where mittens are worn for all sorts of serious work, and where clever knitters are in charge of making things that work.

ROUND TOP OR PICKET-FENCE TOP. The top of the hand is usually shaped in one of these two ways. Ingenious knitters contrive to combine the two shapes.

... Danny went to the bathroom again, apologizing. "It's worse at night," he said. "I'm up at least once an hour, wringing the mitt. That's what the old man used to call it when he'd be pissing over the side of the boat. 'I'm just wringin' out the ol' fishing mitt' ..."

—LINDEN MACINTYRE, *THE BISHOP'S MAN*

Wring one's mitt: of a male, to urinate. Most men went outside to "have a leak," "wring the mitt," urinate, or what have you, before going to bed.

—*DICTIONARY OF NEWFOUNDLAND ENGLISH*

BARREL NIGHT IN MONTREAL

The children and grandchildren of Maud and Charlie Pye of Curling, Newfoundland, now living in Montreal, gathered almost every Saturday night for supper and a game of cards, but one night each fall was uniquely "barrel night." Having retrieved the large barrel from the Port of Montreal, my uncles would manoeuvre it into the kitchen as we reverently gathered round. With a few grunts and pulls of the crowbar the pungent salt cod, smoked capelin and tommy cods would spring free. Small bottles of cherished bakeapples, partridgeberry jam, or a set of embroidered pillowcases would appear under every few layers of fish.

The grandchildren knew that carefully nestled among the fish would be small tissue paper packages reflecting our Nanny's love—our new mittens. A snowflake pattern for the girls and a diamond pattern for the boys and men. Our school teachers often asked where we found such lovely

Mittens for young and old.

mittens. Many colours and sizes came out of that barrel, but each mitt had an odd peak at the top where it was finished off.

Our Nanny never looked at her hands when she knit. In response to our pleas to teach us she would only break out a huge smile and continually repeat "just look now" while her hands soared. Every single one of her 17 grandchildren wore her mittens. They never wore out and were passed from hand to hand and home to home, a constant reminder of her love and our heritage.

— JANICE MAY, OAKVILLE, ON

HELLO GOODBYE
Mittens for Ladies

DEGREE OF DIFFICULTY: ✱✱ TANGLY

Newfoundlanders are always coming and going. We are a well-travelled people.

Much of it has been from one heartbreaking necessity—the need to find work. Many who left never returned, a diaspora that has left deep scars. Stories are told about boys of tender age saying goodbye to their mothers at the top of the stairs in the early morning to go to sea, and never returning home again. Such heartbreak! Many Newfoundlanders continue to travel great distances today, to sustain their families.

Nor can we forget the anguish of an official program of resettling people from remote communities in urban centres, a wound which does not heal. Communities that had held fast to their harbours and fishing grounds for hundreds of years simply withered and disappeared. Beloved homes were torn down, left to rot, or towed over the seas to unfamiliar places. What was the true cost?

There are pleasant comings and goings here too. Accomplished Newfoundlanders often seek their fortunes in faraway places. Others travel far and wide simply for pleasure. There is a great longing in many to experience the quaint and exotic found in other places.

Modern transportation and communication have taken the sting and the finality from our comings and goings, but the poignancy remains. We are always saying hello and goodbye. These mittens say both.

SIZE

Ladies' Medium.
Circumference: 8.5 inches (22 cm).
Length of mitten from beginning of Hello Goodbye pattern to tip: 7 inches (18 cm).
Thumb: 3.25 inches (8 cm). Length of wrist, hand, and thumb is adjustable.

And it's out from St. Leonard's
and out from Toslow,

They'd steam 'cross the bay
with their houses in tow ...

Bound away with their sons
and their daughters.

—GARY O'DRISCOLL, "OUT FROM ST. LEONARD'S"

MATERIALS

Two shades of light worsted weight wool (Group 3), 125 metres Dark (D), 125 metres Light (L). Samples were knit in Briggs and Little Regal 100% wool. 1 set of 4.00 mm double pointed needles. 2 thinner double pointed needles, for 3-needle bind off only (optional). Ring markers.

GAUGE

24 stitches and 28 rows = 4 inches (10 cm).

HELLO GOODBYE CHART FRONT

HELLO GOODBYE CHART PALM

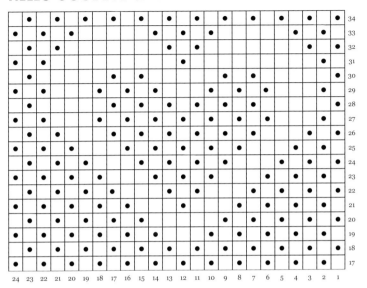

HELLO GOODBYE THUMB GUSSET CHART

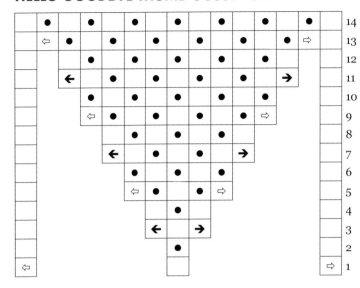

> **"**When the time came for them to be resettled, they didn't shift the house, you know; they took it down. And my grandfather locked himself in his shed and wouldn't come out. **"**

—WILLIAM GOUGH, IN *THE ART OF DAVID BLACKWOOD*

● K1D   Empty square = K1L

→ Make 1 Right with D   ← Make 1 Left with D

⇦ Make 1 Left with L   ⇨ Make 1 Right with L

SALT AND PEPPER PATTERN (S&P)

Worked on an odd number of stitches.

Round 1. (K1D, K1L). Repeat to end of round.

Round 2. (K1L, K1D). Repeat to end of round.

Instructions are for both hands unless otherwise indicated. Work charts from right to left, bottom to top. Always carry D on the left (i.e., ahead) and L on the right to prevent streaks in the work.

With D cast on 36 stitches. Join in a circle, being careful not to twist. Work 24 rounds in (K2, P1) ribbing in a striped pattern of your choice. **Next Round.** With D knit, increasing 13 stitches evenly spaced (49 stitches). Arrange 25 stitches on needle 1 for the front of the mitten. Divide 24 remaining stitches on two needles for palm.

Round 1. Front. Always carrying D on the left, join L and work Round 1 of Hello Goodbye chart for the front of the mitten (25 stitches). **Palm. Right Hand.** K1L, K1D. Place marker. Make 1 right leaning stitch with L. K1L. Make 1 left leaning stitch with L. Place marker. (K1D, K1L) to end of round. **Palm. Left Hand.** (K1L, K1D) until 2 stitches remain in round. Place marker. Make 1 right leaning stitch with L. K1L. Make 1 left leaning stitch with L. Place marker. K1D. There will be 3 L gusset stitches between markers.

This sets up 25 Hello Goodbye stitches on the front of the mitten, S&P stitches on the palm, with thumb gusset stitches inside the markers.

Round 2. Front. Work Round 2 of HG Front chart. **Palm.** Work S&P to marker. Slip marker. Work Round 2 of thumb gusset chart to next marker. Slip marker. Work S&P to end of round.

Continue patterns as established, working successive rounds of thumb gusset chart between markers until Round 14 is complete.

Round 15. Front. Work Round 15 of HG Front chart. **Palm.** Work S&P to marker. Remove marker. Place gusset stitches on a holder. Cast on 1 stitch with L to bridge gap. Remove marker. S&P to end of round (49 stitches).

Round 16. Front. Work Round 16 of HG Front chart. **Palm.** Work S&P to end of round.

Hello Goodbye Classic Mitten, Blue Moon.

Round 17. Front. Work Round 17 of HG Front chart. **Palm.** Work Round 17 of HG Palm chart to end of round.

Continue working successive rounds of HG Front and HG Palm until Round 34 is complete. Work 1 round S&P on all stitches.

Shape Top. Arrange stitches 24, 13, 12. Note that Shaping Round 1 produces adjacent stitches of the same colour at 4 points in the round. These are eliminated on the following round.

Shaping Round 1. Front. K1 with correct S&P colour. SSK with next colour in the sequence. Work S&P until 3 stitches remain on front needle. K2tog with the same colour as the stitch just made. K1 in correct colour of S&P. **Palm.** Work as for front (4 stitches decreased).

Shaping Round 2. Front. K1 in S&P. SSK with next colour in the sequence. S&P to last 3 stitches of front. K2tog with next colour in the sequence. K1 in S&P. **Palm.** Work as for front (4 stitches decreased).

Shaping Round 3. Work in S&P without decreasing.

Repeat shaping rounds 1–3 twice more (25 stitches). Break L leaving a 3-inch tail. Break D leaving a 14-inch tail.

Blue Moon.

3-Needle Bind Off. The hand is finished with a 3-needle bind off on the wrong side of the work.

Place stitches of front on a length of waste yarn. Place stitches of palm on another length of yarn. Turn mitten inside out to work bind off on the wrong side, using the long tail of D. Transfer stitches on yarn to two thinner double pointed needles for easier working. Hold these needles parallel to one another.

With a third double pointed needle of any size and D, K1 from the needle nearest you. Then knit 1 stitch from the front holding needle together with 1 stitch of the opposite colour from the rear holding needle. 2 stitches now on the working needle. Pass first stitch on working needle over second stitch to cast it off. 1 stitch remains on working needle.

Continue to knit together 1 stitch from front and rear holding needles and slipping the first stitch over second stitch on the working needle to cast off. Repeat until 1 stitch remains. Fasten off and darn ends.

Thumb. Transfer thumb stitches from holder to two 4.00 mm double pointed needles. Rejoin yarns and knit these stitches in S&P. With another needle pick up and knit 4 stitches in S&P at the base of the thumb (19 stitches). Work 12 rounds in S&P, or until work reaches tip of thumb.

Thumb Decrease Round 1. (K1 with correct colour in the S&P sequence. SSK with next colour in the sequence. K1 in S&P.) Repeat to end of round, working leftover stitches in S&P. Adjacent stitches in the same colour will be eliminated in the next round.

Thumb Decrease Round 2. (K1 with correct S&P colour. SSK with next colour in the S&P sequence.) Repeat to end of round, working leftover stitches in S&P. Break yarns. Thread through remaining stitches and secure.

Finishing. Darn ends securely. Press lightly under a damp cloth, omitting ribbing.

© Shirley A. Scott 2019

MOOSE CAP
A Traditional Style

DEGREE OF DIFFICULTY: ✱✱ TANGLY

In Newfoundland each fall hunters search out their favourite choice of meat for the winter—moose. Moose is not a native species but was introduced in 1904 as a source of food. They have thrived ever since, providing many a tasty meal.

The moose hunt is so carefully controlled that funny situations arise. A big game licence is required. The gender of the animal to be hunted is designated and noted on each individual licence. Plus the area open for hunting is specified for individuals and very often turns out to be nowhere near

that of the others in the hunting party. What a tangle! A popular comic song tells how one group set about it all.

While not everyone is a hunter, almost everyone loves a moose motif on a cozy cap. This traditional style with turned-up ribbed band features a parade of moose in silhouette, prominently displayed on a timeless salt-and-pepper coloured cap.

SIZE

Adult Medium. Circumference: to fit an average adult head 21 to 22 inches (53 to 56 cm).

MATERIALS

200 metres of medium worsted weight wool (Group 4) in main colour (Ragg). 100 metres Cream. 100 metres Grey. Samples were knit in Briggs and Little Heritage 100% wool using Threaded Grey and White as Ragg. 1 set each of 3.50 mm and 4.50 mm double pointed needles. Stitch markers. 1 sharp darning needle.

Well first to get a moose license,
you apply for six whole years,

At 35 dollars a crack old man,
with a partner for half shares!

And when you get the license,
cock, tis area 28,

Nowhere near civilization,
three hundred miles away!

But I gotta get me moose b'y!

—BUDDY WASISNAME AND THE OTHER FELLERS, "GOTTA GET ME MOOSE B'Y"

GAUGE

8 stitches = 2 inches (5 cm) in stocking stitch using 4.50 mm needles.

Always carry Dark to your left and Light to your right to avoid streaks in work.

The chart is worked right to left, bottom to top, and is repeated 6 times around the circumference of the cap. Place a marker after each repeat of the chart on Round 1. On subsequent rounds slip the markers as you come to them. When the wool not in use is carried for more than 3 stitches,

weave it through at the back of the work at 3-stitch intervals to keep the elasticity of the fairisle moose section of the cap.

Cap Band. Cast on 96 stitches using 3.50 mm double pointed needles and Ragg. Join in a round, being careful not to twist. Place marker. Round 1. Work (K2, P2) rib to end of round. Slip marker. Repeat this round until work measures 3.5 inches (9 cm), increasing 6 stitches evenly spaced on final round.

Change to 4.50 mm double pointed needles. Knit 6 rounds. Break yarn. Knit 1 round with Cream.

Nan
AT YOUR
Side

If your gauge is tighter when knitting with two colours than it is when knitting with a single colour, use needles one size larger in the fairisle portion of the cap only. This maintains even gauge and elasticity. Don't forget to change back to smaller double pointed needles when the fairisle section is done.

MOOSE CHART

17	16	15	14	13	12	11	10	9	8	7	6	5	4	3	2	1	
•	•	•			•				•	•			•	•	•	•	13
•	•	•		•	•		•	•	•		•	•	•	•	•	•	12
•	•	•	•						•	•	•	•	•	•	•		11
•	•	•	•	•	•		•	•	•	•	•	•	•	•	•		10
•	•	•	•	•			•	•	•	•	•	•	•	•			9
•	•	•															8
•	•	•				•									•		7
•	•	•			•	•	•								•		6
•	•	•	•		•	•	•								•		5
•	•	•	•	•				•		•	•		•		•		4
•	•	•	•	•	•		•			•	•		•		•		3
•	•	•	•	•	•		•	•		•	•		•	•			2
•	•	•	•	•	•			•			•			•			1

• K1D   Empty square = K1L

Next Round. Join Grey. (K1 Grey, K1 Cream) to end of round. Work 2 rounds more with Grey.

Moose Chart. Work Moose chart on next 13 rounds as directed. Work 2 rounds Grey.

Next Round. (K1 Grey, K1 Cream) to end of round. Break Grey. Next Round. Work 1 round Cream. Break Cream. Next Round. Rejoin Ragg. Knit 1 round decreasing 2 stitches evenly spaced (100 stitches).

Shape Top. Round 1. (K8, K2tog) to end of round. Round 2. Knit. Round 3. (K7, K2tog) to end of round. Round 4. Knit.

Continue decreasing in this manner, that is, having 1 stitch less between the decreases on alternate rounds until the (K1, K2tog) round is complete. Next Round. (K2tog) to end of round. Break yarn leaving an 8-inch (20 cm) tail. Thread through remaining stitches. Draw up and fasten securely.

Finishing. Darn all ends and trim neatly. Turn cap inside out. Gently press the moose section only.

© Christine LeGrow 2019

STREELY MAID TRIO
Classic Mittens, Trigger Mitts, and Wristers for Ladies

DEGREE OF DIFFICULTY: * EASY DOES IT

In times past a streely maid was a girl whose reputation had seen better days. Any exuberant individuality in dress, attitude, or behaviour might easily earn you this name. Today Newfoundlanders admire vibrant personal expression.

Choose from three options: classic mittens with a picket-fence top, trigger mitts, or fingerless wristers. The fickle climate of our island makes fingerless mitts a blessing even in warmer seasons. In winter people wear these wristers over leather driving gloves to add a bit of élan to their wardrobes. In summer intrepid cyclists and coastal hikers love their warm welcome, especially when chilling fogs descend. In the temperamental weather of spring and fall, wristers may easily be worn every day. Always carry a pair in your pack. When more serious warmth is needed, classic mittens or trigger mitts will do the trick.

Streely Maid is an ideal project for using up oddments of yarn. Pull out the stops when choosing colours for this design and celebrate the bold spirit of streely maids everywhere.

SIZE

Ladies' Medium. Circumference: 8 inches (21 cm). Length of wrister from beginning of Streely Maid pattern: 4.5 inches (12 cm). Length of Classic Mitten and Trigger Mitt from beginning of Streely Maid pattern: 7 inches (18 cm).

MATERIALS

2 or more shades of light worsted weight wool (Group 3), 125 metres of Dark (D), 125 metres of Light (L). Oddments of L may be sufficient. Samples were knit with Briggs and Little Regal 100% wool. 1 set of 4.00 mm double pointed needles. 2 thinner double pointed needles for trigger mitt bind off only (optional). Ring markers.

GAUGE

24 stitches and 28 rows = 4 inches (10 cm).

STREELY MAID CHART (10 stitches x 12 rows)

How to Follow the Streely Maid Chart. Work stitches 1–10 twice horizontally, then stitches 1–5. Work Rounds 1–12 twice vertically. Introduce a new shade of L on Round 7 and the following Round 1 if desired.

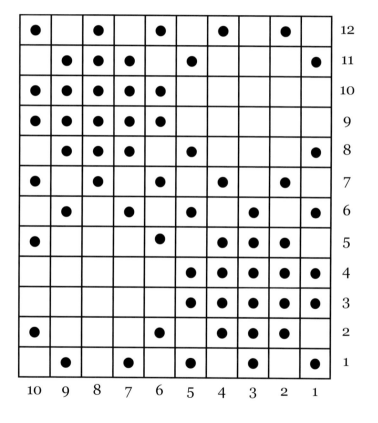

STREELY MAID THUMB GUSSET CHART

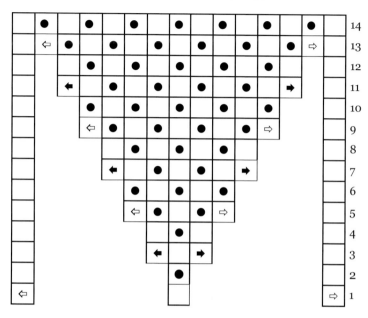

● K1D   Empty square = K1L

➡ Make 1 Right with D   ⬅ Make 1 Left with D

⇦ Make 1 Left with L   ⇨ Make 1 Right with L

SALT AND PEPPER PATTERN (S&P)

Worked over an odd number of stitches.

Round 1. (K1 with D, K1 with L). Repeat to end of round.

Round 2. (K1L, K1D). Repeat to end of round.

Trigger Mitt, Rock 'n' Roll.

TO STREEL

To drag along the ground; to trail or hang untidily.
He was streelin' along behind us all the way home.

STREEL

A dirty, slovenly person, especially a woman. A rag moll.

STREELISH

Also **streely.** Of a woman, untidy or slatternly in appearance.

—*DICTIONARY OF NEWFOUNDLAND ENGLISH*

Classic Mittens.

Wristers.

Work charts from right to left, bottom to top. Always carry D on the left and L on the right to prevent streaks in work. Instructions are for both hands unless otherwise indicated.

Wrist. With the colour of your choice, cast on 36 stitches. Divide evenly on 3 needles and join in a circle, being careful not to twist. Work 24–27 rounds of (K2, P1) ribbing in a striped pattern of your choice, or make three broad tidy jogless stripes as follows.

First Stripe. Work 8 rounds of (K2, P1) ribbing in a colour of your choice. Break yarn. **Second Stripe.** Join another colour of your choice and knit 1 round without ribbing. **Next Round.** Slip first stitch purlwise, rib to end of round. Work 7 rounds more of (K2, P1) rib. Break yarn. **Third Stripe.** Join D and knit 1 round. **Next Round.** Slip first stitch purlwise, rib to end of round. With D work 6 rounds more of (K2, P1) rib.

Next Round. With D knit 1 round, increasing 13 stitches evenly spaced (49 stitches). Arrange work on needles 25 stitches, 12 stitches, 12 stitches. Read **How to Follow the Streely Maid Chart.**

Round 1. Right Hand. Join L, and keeping D ahead (i.e., on the left) throughout, work Round 1 of Streely chart on 25 stitches for front of hand. **Palm.** K1L, K1D. Place marker. M1R with L. K1L. M1L with L. Place marker. (K1D, K1L) to last stitch. K1D. There will be 3 L stitches between markers. **Left Hand.** Join L and, keeping D ahead (i.e., on the left) throughout, work Round 1 of Streely chart for 25 stitches for front. **Palm.** (K1L, K1D) until 2 stitches remain in round. Place marker. M1R with L. K1L. M1L with L. Place marker. K1D. There will be 3 L stitches between markers.

Both Hands. This sets up 25 Streely stitches on the front, 24 S&P stitches on the palm, and Round 1 of the thumb gusset with its 2 outline stitches between the markers.

Round 2. Work Round 2 of Streely chart on front. **Palm.** Work in S&P to marker, slip marker. Work Round 2 of thumb gusset

Streely Maid Wrister, Lupins.

chart to next marker, slip marker. Work S&P to end of round.

Continue in patterns as established until thumb gusset Round 14 is complete, finishing the round in S&P. There will be 15 gusset stitches between markers.

Next Round. Work next round of Streely pattern on front. **Palm.** Work S&P to marker, remove marker. Place gusset stitches on a piece of waste yarn, remove marker. Cast on 1 stitch with correct colour of S&P to bridge gap. Work S&P to end of round (49 stitches).

Continue working Streely Maid on the front and S&P on the palm until 24 Streely pattern rounds are complete, finishing the round in S&P.

For Classic Mittens, proceed to Classic Mittens Only. For Trigger Mitts, proceed to Trigger Mitts Only.

WRISTERS ONLY
Top Trim. With the colour of your choice knit 1 round. **Next Round.** (K2, P1, K2, P2tog) to end of round (42 stitches). **Next Round.** (K2, P1) rib to end of round. Cast off in ribbing.

Nan AT YOUR Side

Casting Off in Ribbing. Nan swears by this finishing touch for the trim on her wristers. It's painless. For a smooth join with no stair steps, slip the first stitch to be cast off purlwise instead of knitting it. Then cast off this and all other stitches normally until 1 stitch remains to be worked. Slip this last stitch purlwise, then cast it off.

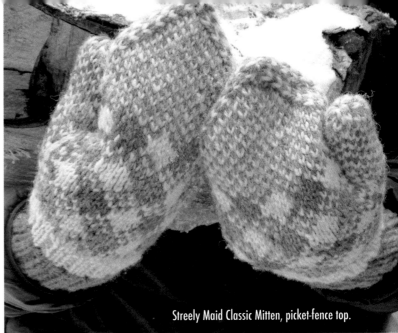

Streely Maid Classic Mitten, picket-fence top.

Thumb Trim. Transfer gusset stitches to 2 double pointed needles. Join the colour of your choice and knit these stitches. Pick up and knit 3 stitches at the base of the thumb (18 stitches). Arrange work on 3 needles and work 2 rounds of (K2, P1) rib. Cast off in rib.

CLASSIC MITTENS ONLY

Next Round. Work in S&P to end of round. Work 11 rounds more in S&P, or until work reaches the tip of the little finger.

Shape Picket-Fence Top. Decreases are made 1 stitch from the edge at 4 points in the round, positioned as on the toe of a sock. Decreases are made on every round.

Shaping Round 1. Front. With Streely facing, K1 in correct colour. SSK with the next colour in the sequence. Resume S&P on the next stitch (having made 2 adjacent stitches of the same colour). Work in S&P until 3 stitches remain on front. K2tog in the same colour as the stitch just made. Work last stitch in correct colour of sequence. **Palm.** As front.

Shaping Round 2. Front. K1, SSK in next colour in the sequence. S&P until 3 stitches remain on front. K2tog in next colour in the sequence, K1. **Palm.** As front. Correct colour sequence is restored.

Repeat these 2 shaping rounds until 9 stitches remain. Break yarns. Thread one into a darning needle and pass through remaining stitches. Pull tight and fasten. Proceed to Thumb.

TRIGGER MITTS ONLY

Next Round. Work in S&P to end of round. **Left Hand Only.** Break yarns.

Both Hands. Reserve Trigger Finger Stitches. With Streely facing, at the same edge of the mitten as the thumb, place 8 stitches from the front and corresponding 8 stitches from the palm on holders for the trigger finger.

Right Hand. With Streely facing, work in S&P to the gap. Cast on 2 stitches in pattern to bridge gap. Work in S&P to end of round (35 stitches).

Left Hand. With Streely facing, rejoin yarns. Work S&P on the front and palm to the gap. Cast on 2 stitches in pattern to bridge gap. Note new beginning of round (35 stitches).

Both Hands. Arrange stitches (17, 9, 9). Knit 11 rounds more in S&P, or until work reaches the tip of the little finger.

Shape Top. Decreases are made 1 stitch from the edge at 4 points in the round, positioned as on the toe of a sock. Two decrease rounds are followed by a round with no decreases to produce the rounded top.

Shaping Round 1. Front. With Streely facing, K1 in correct colour. SSK with the next colour in the sequence. Resume S&P on the next stitch (having made 2 adjacent stitches of the same colour). Work in pattern until 3 stitches remain on front. K2tog in the same colour as the stitch just made. Work last stitch in correct colour. **Palm.** As front.

*Streely Maid Trigger Mitt,
Winter Dawn.*

Shaping Round 2.
Front. K1, SSK in next colour in the sequence. S&P until 3 stitches remain on front. K2tog in next colour in the sequence, K1. **Palm.** As front. Correct colour sequence is restored.

Shaping Round 3. Work in S&P without decreasing.

Repeat these 3 shaping rounds once more, ending with Round 3 (19 stitches). Break yarns, leaving a long tail with one colour.

3-Needle Bind Off. The hand is finished with a 3-needle bind off on the wrong side of the work.

Place stitches of front on a length of waste yarn. Place stitches of palm on another length of yarn. Turn mitten inside out to work bind off on the wrong side using the long tail.

Return stitches on holders to two thinner double pointed needles for easier working. Hold these needles parallel to one another, the needle with the larger number of stitches nearest you. With a third double pointed needle and the long tail, K1 from the front holding needle. Then knit 1 stitch from this needle together with 1 stitch of the opposite colour from the rear needle. 2 stitches now on the working needle. Pass first stitch on working needle over second stitch to cast it off. 1 stitch remains on the working needle. Continue to knit together 1 stitch from front and rear holding needles and slipping the first stitch over second stitch on the working needle to cast off. Repeat until 1 stitch remains on working needle. Fasten off and darn ends. Turn work right side out.

Trigger Finger. Transfer stitches from front holder to a double pointed needle. Place stitches from palm on a double pointed needle.

Right Trigger Finger. With Streely facing, rejoin yarns and work in S&P to the gap. Pick up and knit 3 stitches in correct S&P sequence from the base of the hand (19 stitches).

Left Trigger Finger. With Streely facing, rejoin yarns, working stitches of front in S&P. Pick up and knit 3 stitches in correct colour sequence from base of hand. Work palm stitches in S&P (19 stitches).

Both Hands. Note beginning of round. Divide stitches on 3 double pointed needles and work 14 rounds more of S&P, or until work reaches the tip of the index finger.

Finger Decrease Round 1. (K1 with correct colour in the S&P sequence, SSK with next colour in the sequence, K1 in S&P), repeat to end of round, working any leftover stitches in S&P. Adjacent stitches in the same colour will be eliminated in the next round.

Finger Decrease Round 2. (K1 with correct S&P colour, SSK with next colour in the S&P sequence) to end of round working any leftover stitches in S&P. Break yarns. Thread through remaining stitches and secure.

Thumb. Transfer thumb stitches from holder to two double pointed needles. Rejoin yarns and knit these stitches in S&P. With another needle pick up and knit 4 stitches in S&P at the base of the thumb (19 stitches). Note beginning of round. Work 12 rounds more in S&P, or until work reaches the tip of the thumb. Work Finger Decrease Rounds 1–2.

Finishing. Darn ends securely. Press lightly, omitting ribbing.

© Shirley A. Scott 2019

Streely Maid Wrister, Blue Moon.

TRINITY
Cap for Ladies

DEGREE OF DIFFICULTY: ✱ ✱ TANGLY

The historic town of Trinity (48.36°N, 53.35°W), located in the Trinity Bight area of Trinity Bay, has been settled for centuries. It was named by Portuguese explorer Gaspar Corte-Real when he made landfall on Trinity Sunday in 1500 or 1501 CE. A visit to Trinity is like stepping into a pretty postcard from long ago. Historically significant buildings dot the town. Church steeples, pristine houses with traditional architectural details, the Green Family Forge, picket fences surrounding exquisite gardens, and a marina full of brightly painted boats are a feast for the eyes. The famous New Founde Lande Trinity pageant, presented by the Rising Tide Theatre Company, brings the history of the area to life every summer.

This intricately textured cap is worked flat in a modified Trinity stitch, then seamed. Neat seaming will make it reversible.

SIZE

Ladies' Medium. Circumference: 21–22 inches (53–56 cm).

MATERIALS

200 metres worsted weight wool (Group 4). 1 pair of very strong needles size 3.50 mm, 1 pair of very strong needles size 4.50 mm. Metal needles are preferred. Less strong needles may break. 1 sharp darning needle. Pins. Samples were knit with Briggs and Little Heritage 100% wool.

GAUGE

8 stitches = 2 inches (5 cm) in stocking stitch using 4.50 mm needles.

MODIFIED TRINITY STITCH

KPBK. Knit into the front of the next stitch then purl into the back of the same stitch then knit into the same stitch before slipping it off the needle.

Row 1. Purl.
Row 2 (P3tog, KPBK). Repeat to last 3 stitches. P3tog.
Row 3. Purl.
Row 4. (KPBK, P3tog). Repeat to last stitch. KPBK.

BIGHT

A bend in the coast forming an open bay.

—Merriam-Webster

In Newfoundland bays, coves and deep indentations where the sea creeps into the land are often called tickles, guts, arms, sounds, or fjords. Our immense coastline is speckled with all of these.

Trinity window.

Nan
AT YOUR
Side

Sew the seam the same way as sewing up a stuffed turkey. Check as you go. If you catch each edge perfectly and darn in the ends with precision, you will have a reversible cap. One side will feature Modified Trinity stitch with a stocking stitch crown, the other a Twig stitch with reverse stocking stitch crown.

Trinity, reverse
stocking stitch crown.

With 3.50 needles cast on 111 stitches. **Row 1.** (K1 through back of loop, P1). Repeat to last stitch K1. **Row 2.** (P1, K1 through back of loop). Repeat to last stitch, P1. Continue in ribbing until work from cast on edge measures 4 inches (10 cm).

Change to size 4.50 mm needles and repeat Rows 1–4 of Modified Trinity Stitch until the patterned section measures 4.5 inches (11.5 cm).

Shape Crown. With 3.50 mm needles (K9, K2tog) 9 times, K9, K3tog (100 stitches). Purl 1 row.

Decrease Top. Row 1. (K8, K2tog). Repeat to end of row. **Row 2.** Purl. **Row 3.** (K7, K2tog). Repeat to end of row. **Row 4.** Purl. Continue decreasing in the manner, having 1 stitch less between the decreases on alternate rows until the (K1, K2tog) row is complete. Purl 1 row. **Next Row.** (K2tog) to end of row.

Break yarn, leaving a tail approximately 20 inches (51 cm) long. Thread the darning needle and draw through remaining stitches. Draw up and fasten securely.

Finishing. With the wrong side of work facing, pin the seam together at the last row of ribbing and the last row of Modified Trinity Stitch, to match the sections. Place another pin halfway between. Stitch sides together, taking care to catch the first and last stitches of each row, particularly the bumpy patterned edge. Darn ends and trim neatly.

© Christine LeGrow 2019

TICKLE COVE
Beanie for Four Seasons

DEGREE OF DIFFICULTY: * EASY DOES IT

Tickle Cove is a picturesque spot with unusual landscape and geological features. From the dramatic sea arch to the purple and pink rocks at its coast, it is a treat for the senses. Tickle Cove Pond is locally famous in a song by the same name. Performed and recorded by many, it tells the dramatic tale of Kit the Mare and the attempts to save her, a valuable lesson to learn when venturing onto frozen ponds. Where will you find this intriguing place? On the Bonavista Peninsula (48.58°N, 53.48°W). Tickle Cove plants a forever memory in all those who visit.

The Tickle Cove Beanie is made for year-round wear in Newfoundland. Neat and tidy with gently textured arches, it is a quick knit and tucks easily into a pocket when needed.

SIZE

Gauge determines size. Beanie may be lengthened.

Small. Circumference: 19–20 inches (51–53 cm), knit in light worsted weight (Group 3) yarn with 3.75 mm needles.
Large. Circumference: 22–23 inches (56–58 cm), knit in medium worsted weight (Group 4) yarn with 4.00 mm needles.

MATERIALS

Small. 125 metres light worsted weight (Group 3) wool. 1 set 3.25 mm double pointed needles. 1 set 3.75 mm double pointed needles.

Large. 200 metres medium worsted weight (Group 4) wool. 1 set 3.50 mm double pointed needles. 1 set 4.00 mm double pointed needles.

1 sharp darning needle. Stitch markers.

GAUGE

Small. 10 stitches = 2 inches (7.5 cm) in light worsted weight (Group 3) yarn using 3.75 mm needles.

Large. 9 stitches = 2 inches (7.5 cm) in medium worsted weight (Group 4) yarn using 4.00 mm needles.

TICKLE COVE ARCH CHART

How to Follow the Tickle Cove Arch Chart. There are 6 arches around the circumference, separated by two knit stitches. Work chart vertically twice.

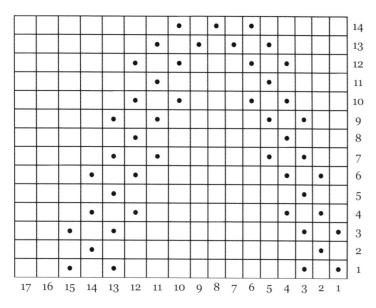

• Purl   Empty square = Knit

In days of old the sturdy Newfoundland pony with a handmade cart hauled firewood year-round, especially over frozen ground and ponds in winter. A famous 19th-century song paints the picture:

In cuttin' and haulin' in frost and in snow

*We're up against troubles
that few people know.*

It's only by courage and patience and grit

*And eatin' plain food
that we keep ourselves fit.*

The hard and the easy we take as they come

*And when ponds freeze over
we shorten our runs.*

To hurry my haulin' with Spring comin' on

*I near lost me mare out
on Tickle Cove Pond.*

—MARK WALKER, "TICKLE COVE POND"

Beanie Band. With smaller double pointed needles and yarn of choice, cast on 93 stitches. Join in a round, being careful not to twist. **Round 1.** (K1, P1). Repeat to last stitch. K1. **Round 2.** (P1, K1). Repeat to last stitch. P1. Repeat these 2 rounds 4 times more. **Next Round.** As Round 1, increasing 9 stitches evenly spaced (102 stitches).

Arch Section. Change to larger double pointed needles. Work chart from right to left, bottom to top.

Next Round. (Work Round 1 of Arch Chart on stitches 1–17. Place marker.) Repeat to end of round. Continue working successive rounds of Tickle Cove Arch until 28 rounds are complete.

Next Round. Knit, removing sectional markers as you come to them. Knit 5 rounds more.

Shape Top. Round 1. (K2tog, K13, SSK). Place marker. Repeat to end of round. **Round 2.** Knit, slipping markers. **Round 3.** (K2tog, K11, SSK, slip marker). Repeat to end of round. **Round 4.** Knit.

Continue decreasing in this manner on alternate rounds

Nan AT YOUR Side

For those who prefer to wear a cap pulled down to the eyebrows and totally covering the earlobes, knit 4 extra rounds before beginning the top shaping.

until 18 stitches remain, ending with a knit round and removing sectional markers on the last round. **Next Round.** (K2tog, SSK), repeat to last 2 stitches of round, K2tog. Break yarn leaving a 12-inch (30 cm) tail. Thread through remaining stitches and fasten off.

Finishing. Darn ends. Turn inside out and lightly press over the end of an ironing board, omitting the ribbing.

© Christine LeGrow 2019

Tickle Cove arch.

Tickle Cove beach.

SALT AND PEPPER
Caps for Adults

DEGREE OF DIFFICULTY: * EASY DOES IT

This Salt and Pepper Cap, as it is known locally, gained great popularity during the career of Newfoundland musician Harry Hibbs. A singer of traditional songs, he always wore a woven newsboy cap perched atop his head when he performed. At some point during his years of fame, knitters started making a version of the Harry Hibbs signature cap at home, and everyone wanted one. Roughly typed and scribbled patterns popped up everywhere. Yarn companies jumped on the bandwagon a little later. Knit on straight needles, the earliest version was a basic tam with a "bib" or "peak" sewn on and a button attached at the crown. Later a coin was sometimes inserted inside a knitted square and sewn on instead of a button. Every man had one and wore it just like Harry, perched atop his head, ears frozen on a winter's day.

Our pattern is an updated variation of Harry's original. Knit in the round, we have made it deeper for greater ear protection and not as broad. Unlike Harry's, our cap is most definitely unisex.

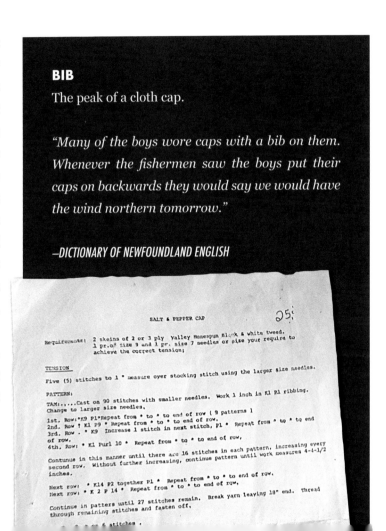

BIB

The peak of a cloth cap.

"Many of the boys wore caps with a bib on them. Whenever the fishermen saw the boys put their caps on backwards they would say we would have the wind northern tomorrow."

—*DICTIONARY OF NEWFOUNDLAND ENGLISH*

SALT & PEPPER CAP 25¢

Requirements: 2 skeins of 2 or 3 ply Valley Homespun Black & white tweed. 1 pr. of size 9 and 1 pr. size 7 needles or size your require to achieve the correct tension;

TENSION

Five (5) stitches to 1 " measure over stocking stitch using the larger size needles.

PATTERN:

TAM:.....Cast on 90 stitches with smaller needles. Work 1 inch in K1 P1 ribbing. Change to larger size needles.

1st. Row: *K9 P1*Repeat from * to * end of row (9 patterns)
2nd. Row : K1 P9 * Repeat from * to * to end of row.
3rd. Row . * K9 Increase 1 stitch in next stitch, P1 * Repeat from * to * to end of row.
4th. Row: * K1 Purl 10 * Repeat from * to * to end of row,

Contunue in this manner until there are 16 stitches in each pattern, increasing every second row. Without further increasing, continue pattern until work measures 4-4-1/2 inches.

Next row: * K14 P2 together P1 * Repeat from * to * to end of row,
Next row: * K 2 P 14 * Repeat from * to * to end of row,

Continue in patters until 27 stitches remain. Break yarn leaving 18" end. Thread through remaining stitches and fasten off.

.... 6 stitches .

SIZE

Young Adult. Circumference: 21 inches (53.5 cm).

Medium Adult. Circumference: 22 inches (56 cm). This size is slightly deeper at the crown.

MATERIALS

200 metres medium worsted weight wool (Group 4). Samples were knit using Briggs and Little Heritage 100% wool in Threaded Grey and White. 1 set 3.50 mm double pointed needles. 1 set 4.50 mm double pointed needles. Sharp darning needle. Safety pins.

GAUGE

15 stitches = 3 inches (7.5 cm) when worked in stocking stitch using 4.50 mm needles.

HARRY HIBBS (1942–1989)

He was born on Bell Island, Conception Bay, in the Dominion of Newfoundland. Although he lived and worked largely on the mainland of Canada, he is considered Bell Island's sweetheart son. A musical legend in his own time, his unique style gained him great popularity. He recorded many albums, had many gold records, and his own television show, where he entertained his fans by singing and playing accordion, always wearing his salt and pepper cap. Some of Harry's most popular recorded songs are "The Bell Island Song," "Between Two Trees," "The Cliffs of Baccalieu," and dozens of traditional folk songs from other places such as "Black Velvet Band" and "Roses Are Blooming."

This pattern is written for the Young Adult size. Changes for Medium Adult follow where necessary. If only one number is given, it applies to both sizes.

Using 3.50 double pointed needles cast on 90 (94) stitches and join in a round, being careful not to twist.

RIBBING

(K1, P1) to end of round. Repeat this round until the ribbed band measures 1.25 inches (3 cm). 1.50 inches (4 cm). Change to 4.50 mm double pointed needles.

Make 1 (M1) can mean a lot of things in knitting. Here it means make one stitch by picking up the horizontal loop lying in front of the next stitch and knitting into the back of it before slipping it off the needle.

Young Adult Only. Rounds 1–2. (K9, P1). Repeat to end of round. **Round 3. Increase Round.** (K9, M1, P1.) Repeat to end of round (99 stitches).

Medium Only. Rounds 1–2. K9, P1. *(K10, P1) twice. (K9, P1) twice*. Repeat from * to * once. **Round 3. Increase Round.** K9, M1, P1. *(K10, P1) twice. (K9, M1, P1) twice*. Repeat from * to * once (99 stitches).

Both Sizes. Round 4. (K10, P1). Repeat to end of round. **Round 5.** (K10, M1, P1). Repeat to end of round. **Round 6.** (K11, P1). Repeat to end of round.

Continue in this manner, making one stitch before each purl stitch on every alternate round until there are 14 (15) knit stitches between each purled stitch.

Maintaining this pattern of the purl stitch separating the knit stitches, continue without increasing until work measures 4.25 (4.5) inches from cast on edge.

SHAPE TOP

Medium Only. Next Round. (K13, P2tog, P1). Next Round. (K13, P2).

Both Sizes. Decrease Round 1. (K12, P2tog, P1). Repeat to end of round. **Decrease Round 2.** (K12, P2). Repeat to end of round. **Decrease Round 3.** (K11, P2tog, P1). Repeat to end of round. **Decrease Round 4.** (K11, P2). Repeat to end of round.

Continue decreasing in this manner, having 1 knit stitch less between the purl stitches on alternate rounds, until the (K1, P2tog, P1) round is complete.

Next Round. K2tog to last stitch, K1. Break yarn leaving a 12-inch tail. Thread through remaining stitches. Draw up and fasten securely.

Peak. Knit flat.
Using 3.50 mm needles cast on 6 stitches.

Row 1. K3, M1, K3. **Row 2.** K3, P1, K3. **Row 3.** K3, M1, K1, M1, K3. **Row 4.** K3, P3, K3. **Row 5.** K4, M1, K1, M1, K4. **Row 6.** K3, P5, K3.

Continue increasing in this manner, with an M1 stitch on either side of the centre stitch on alternate rows while keeping the 3 knit stitches on both sides, until there are 23 (25) stitches on the needle. Work 21 (23) rows without increasing.

Begin Decreasing. Row 1. K9 (10), SSK, K1, K2tog, K9 (10). **Row 2.** K3, purl to last 3 stitches, K3. **Row 3.** K8 (9), SSK, K1, K2tog, K8 (9). **Row 4.** As Row 2.

Continue decreasing on alternate rows until 9 stitches

remain on the needles. **Both Sizes. Next Row.** K3, S1, K2tog, pass slipped stitch over, K3. **Next Row.** K3, P1, K3. **Next Row.** K3, S1, K1, pass slipped stitch over, K2 (6 stitches). Cast off. Break yarn, leaving a 24-inch tail. Stitch both edges of the peak together.

Finishing. To attach the peak to the cap, line up the garter stitch edge to the cast on edge of the band. Using a few safety pins, centre it approximately half way round. Beginning with and including the cast on and cast off borders, carefully sew in place on the underside without stretching or puckering. Break yarn and darn ends. Darn remaining ends. Press the peak and cap lightly, omitting the ribbing on the band.

Button Cover. Using 3.50 mm needles cast on 8 stitches. **Row 1.** Knit. **Row 2.** Purl. Repeat these 2 rows 3 times more. **Row 9.** Knit. Cast off purlwise.

Break yarn, leaving a 12-inch tail. Using a sharp darning needle and running stitch, gather up the stitches around the 4 sides. Place a 25-cent piece in the centre of the purl side,

Newfoundland was a British colony from 1610 until 1854, when it was designated a Crown colony. In 1907 it became a British dominion, until it joined Canada in 1949. It had its own currency, including the Newfoundland pound, later the Newfoundland dollar and several silver coins, one being the silver 25-cent piece. These coins are highly collectible today.

There was much raucous debate when deciding to join or not to join Canada. Numerous photos from that era show the storming of the Colonial Building, when hundreds of the men wore woven, tweed newsboy caps imported from the British Isles.

draw up the edges and fasten securely. Sew this button firmly to the cap.

VIVE LA ROSE
Classic Mittens and Trigger Mitts

DEGREE OF DIFFICULTY: ✱ ✱ ✱ Over the Wharf

French history and influence are strong on the west coast of the island of Newfoundland. Émile Benoît interpreted this legacy through music and song. An accomplished fiddle player who entertained as a hobby, he was a fisherman by trade but became a fulltime entertainer after he retired from the fishery. Wherever he entertained, songs and melodies echoed into the night air, none more poignantly than "Vive La Rose," a French folk song of unrequited love. Émile enriched his island home and indeed the whole of Canada and the world with his fiddle playing, storytelling, and song. His mission was, in his own words, "to make people laugh and to make people happy. That's my life ... I would toss myself in the sea if it would make you laugh enough. Yep. And I don't know how to swim."

Now you can knit a romantic pair of mittens or trigger mitts in several sizes by simply changing the yarn and needles used.

SIZE

Classic Mitten and Trigger Mitt. Size M. Circumference: 8.75 inches (22 cm). Length of mitten and trigger mitt from beginning of Vive La Rose pattern to tip: 7.25 inches (18.5 cm). Thumb: 2.50 inches (6.50 cm). Length is adjustable. Use light worsted weight (Group 3) wool.

Trigger Mitt Only. Size L. Circumference: 9.25 inches (23.5 cm). Length from beginning of Vive La Rose pattern to tip: 7.75 inches (20 cm). Thumb: 2.75 inches (7cm). Length is adjustable. Use medium worsted weight wool (Group 4).

For some people these phrases all sound similar though they are not at all the same. *Vive la rose* means long live the rose. *Vie en rose* is a shade of bright pink. *La vie en rose* means seeing life through rose-coloured glasses.

Trigger mitts.

MATERIALS

Classic Mitten and Trigger Mitt. Size M. 150 metres each of light worsted weight wool (Group 3) in Dark (D) and Light (L). 1 set 3.25 mm double pointed needles. Samples were knit using Briggs and Little Regal 100% wool.

Trigger Mitt Only. Size L. 150 metres each of medium worsted weight wool (Group 4) in Dark (D) and Light (L). 1 set 3.50 double pointed needles. Samples were knit using Briggs and Little Heritage 100% wool.

Both Sizes. Stitch markers, stitch holders, and a sharp darning needle.

GAUGE

11 stitches = 2 inches (5 cm) worked in light worsted weight wool in stocking stitch using 3.25 mm needles.

9 stitches = 2 inches (5 cm) worked in medium worsted weight wool in stocking stitch using 3.50 mm needles.

Vive La Rose Trigger Mitt.

Vive La Rose Classic Mitten, First Light.

VIVE LA ROSE CHART (VR)

How to Follow the Vive La Rose Chart.

Classic Mitten. Work Rounds 1–8 four times, then Round 1 once (33 rounds on the front of the mitten).

Trigger Mitt. Work Rounds 1–8 three times, then Round 1 once (25 rounds on the front of the mitten).

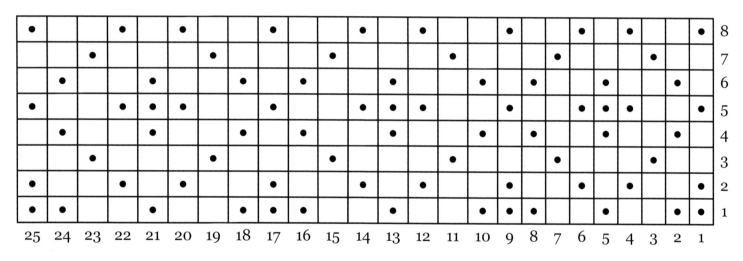

- K1D   Empty square = K1L

VIVE LA ROSE THUMB GUSSET CHART

- K1D

⇐ Make 1 Left with L

Empty square = K1L

⇒ Make 1 Right with L

SALT AND PEPPER PATTERN (S&P)

Worked on an odd number of stitches.

Round 1: (K1D, K1L). Repeat to end of round.

Round 2: (K1L, K1D). Repeat to end of round.

Trigger Mitt and Classic Mitten, First Light.

Please read all instructions before casting on. Instructions are written for the right hand of the Classic Mitten. Changes for the Trigger Mitt or for size are identified.

Wrist. With the correct size of needles and yarn for your choice of design and D cast on 38 stitches. Join in round, being careful not to twist. **Round 1.** (K1, P1) repeat to end of round. Continue in ribbing until work measures 3 inches (Trigger Mitt 3.5 inches, 9 cm), increasing 11 stitches evenly spaced on the last round (49 stitches).

Right Hand Only. Arrange stitches as follows. Needle 1. 25 stitches (front of the mitten). Needles 2 and 3. 12 stitches each. Work charts from bottom to top, right to left. Always carry D on the left and L on the right to prevent streaks in the work.

Round 1. Join L. Work Round 1 of VR chart for front of the mitten. Place marker. Work Round 1 of thumb gusset chart (increase round). Place marker. Work Round 1 of S&P pattern to end of round (palm 19 stitches). **Round 2.** Work Round 2 of VR chart on front. Slip marker. Work Round 2 of thumb gusset chart. Slip marker. Work Round 2 of S&P pattern to end of round. Continue in this manner working successive rounds of VR chart on the front, thumb gusset chart and S&P pattern on the palm, until Round 17 is complete.

Right Hand Round 18. Work Round 18 of VR. Remove marker. K1D over the Dark outline stitch. Slip 15 thumb gusset stitches on a thread to be worked later. Cast on 5 stitches in correct colour sequence to bridge the gap. K1D over the final dark outline stitch. Remove marker. Work S&P pattern to end of round (51 stitches). Thumb gusset is complete and the 2 D outline stitches have now become part of the main section of the mitten. Proceed to Both Hands.

Left Hand Only. Place stitches on the needles as follows. **Needle 1.** 25 stitches (front of the mitten). **Needles 2 and 3.** 12 stitches each. **Round 1.** Join L. Work Round 1 of VR chart on needle 1. Work Round 1 of S&P until 5 stitches remain in round. Place marker. Work Round 1 of thumb gusset chart (increase round) on these stitches. Place marker. **Round 2.** Work Round 2 of VR on front. Work S&P to marker. Slip marker. Work Round 2 of thumb gusset chart. Slip marker. Left hand thumb gusset is now positioned. Continue to work in same manner as right mitten, but with these reversed shapings, until Round 17 is complete.

Left Hand Round 18. Work Round 18 of VR chart. Work S&P to marker. Remove marker. K1 in correct colour sequence. Slip 15 thumb gusset stitches on a thread to be worked later. Cast on 5 stitches in correct colour sequence to bridge the gap. K1D over the final D outline stitch. Remove marker (51 stitches). Thumb gusset is complete. Proceed to Both Hands.

Both Hands. Continue to work successive rounds of VR chart on the front of the mitten and S&P on the palm until (Trigger Mitt: Round 25) (Classic Mitt: Round 33) is complete. **Classic Mitten Only.** Work 4 rounds more in S&P. Adjust length if required by working additional rounds of S&P. Proceed to Shape Top.

Right Trigger Mitt. Index Finger. Break yarns. Place 7 stitches from the end of needle 1 on a spare needle. Place the first 7 stitches from needle 2 on a spare needle. Slip the remaining 37 stitches from the front and palm on a thread to

be worked later. Keeping S&P pattern correct, rejoin yarns and work the 7 stitches on needle 1 (front). Work the 7 stitches on needle 2. Using a third needle cast on 5 stitches in correct colour sequence to bridge the gap. Join these 19 stitches in a round. Work 15 rounds or desired length in S&P pattern. **Finger Decrease Round 1.** (Knit first stitch in correct colour sequence. SSK with next colour. K1 with the same colour as the stitch just worked.) Repeat to end of round, knitting any remaining stitches in S&P. **Finger Decrease Round 2.** (K1, SSK) in S&P, working any remaining stitches in S&P. Break yarns leaving a D tail approximately 6 inches (15 cm) long. Thread through remaining stitches, tighten, and fasten securely.

Right Trigger Mitt. Upper Hand. Slip the 37 stitches from the thread to 3 needles as follows. Needle 1: 18 stitches (front of the mitten). Needles 2 and 3 share 19 palm stitches. With VR facing rejoin yarns. Work S&P to index finger. Pick up and knit 4 stitches in the correct colour sequence at the base of the index finger. Continue in S&P pattern to end of round (41 stitches). Work 15 rounds or desired length in S&P. Slip 2 stitches from the beginning of needle 2 onto the end of needle 1. There are now 20 stitches on needle 1 (front of the mitten). Needles 2 and 3 share 21 palm stitches.

Proceed to Both Hands. Shape Top.

Want more colour options? Try keeping the wrist and outline of the thumb gusset Dark as before but use this pattern chart instead.

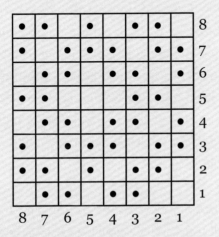

• K1D   Empty square = K1 Light

Always keep D to the left and L to the right to prevent colour streaks in your work. Work chart right to left, bottom to top. Repeat stitches 1 to 8 three times then stitch 1 once (25 stitches). **Classic Mitten.** Repeat rows 1 to 8 four times then row 1 once (33 rows for front of the Classic Mitten). **Trigger Mitt.** repeat rows 1 to 8 three times, then row 1 once (25 rows for the front).

Nan
AT YOUR
Side

Left Trigger Mitt. Index Finger. Round 26. Work S&P on first 7 stitches of needle 1. Slip the next 37 stitches onto a thread to be worked later. 7 stitches remain on the third needle. With VR facing, and using another needle, cast on 5 stitches in correct colour sequence to bridge the gap. Needle 3. Work 7 stitches in S&P. Join in a round. Complete left index finger as right index finger.

Left Trigger Mitt. Upper Hand. With VR facing, slip 18 stitches from the thread to needle 1. Place first 10 palm stitches on a second needle. Slip the remaining 9 palm stitches to a third needle. Rejoin yarns. Pick up and knit 4 stitches in correct colour sequence at the base of the index finger (41 stitches). Work 15 rounds more or desired length in S&P. **Next Round.** Work in (S&P) until 2 stitches remain in round. Slip these 2 stitches to the beginning of needle 1. Continue in S&P to end of round (needle 1: 20 stitches, needles 2 and 3 share 21 palm stitches). Proceed to Both Hands. Shape Top.

Both Hands. Shape Top. Decreases are made 1 stitch in from the edge at 4 points in the round. On odd-numbered rounds, decreasing will create two adjacent stitches in the same colour. On even-numbered rounds, these stitches will be worked together, restoring the correct colour sequence.

Shaping Round 1. Needle 1. K1 in correct colour. SSK with the next colour in the sequence. Resume pattern on the next stitch, having made 2 adjacent stitches of the same colour. Work in pattern until 3 stitches remain before the end of the needle. K2tog in the same colour as the stitch just made. Work last stitch in the correct colour. **Needle 2.** K1, SSK with the next colour in the sequence. Work in pattern to the end of the needle. **Needle 3.** Work in pattern until 3 stitches remain before the end of the round. K2tog in the same colour as the stitch just made. K1 in correct colour. **Shaping Round 2. Needle 1.** K1 in S&P. SSK with next colour in the sequence. S&P until 3 stitches remain on needle. K2tog with next colour in the sequence. K1 in S&P. **Needle 2.** K1. SSK with the next colour in the sequence. Work in pattern to the end of the needle. **Needle 3.** Work in pattern until 3 stitches remain before the end of the round. K2tog in the next colour in the sequence. K1 in correct colour. Repeat these two shaping rounds until (Classic Mitten 19) (Trigger Mitt 17) stitches remain. Proceed to 3-Needle Bind Off.

Both Hands. 3-Needle Bind Off. The hand is finished with a 3-needle bind off on the wrong side of the work. Place stitches of front on a length of waste yarn. Place stitches of palm on another length of yarn. Turn mitten inside out to work bind off on the wrong side, using the long tail. Return stitches on holders to 2 double pointed needles. Hold these needles parallel to one another, the needle with the larger

number of stitches nearest you. With a third double pointed needle and the long tail, K1 from the holding needle nearest you. Then knit 1 stitch from this needle together with 1 stitch of the opposite colour from the back needle. 2 stitches now on the working needle. Pass first stitch on working needle over second stitch to cast it off. 1 stitch remains on the working needle. Continue to knit together 1 stitch from front and back holding needles and slipping the first stitch over second stitch on the working needle to bind off. Repeat until 1 stitch remains on the working needle. Fasten and secure.

Both Hands. Thumb. Place the 15 thumb stitches on 2 needles. Rejoin yarns. Using a third needle, pick up and knit 6 stitches in correct colour sequence at the base of the mitten (21 stitches). Work thumb in S&P for 15 rounds or desired length. Work Finger Decrease Rounds 1 and 2.

Finishing. Carefully darn in all ends, trim neatly. Press under a damp cloth, omitting ribbing.

© Christine LeGrow 2019

PLAISANCE
Gloves for Ladies

DEGREE OF DIFFICULTY: ✱ ✱ ✱ Over the Wharf

Plaisance is the old French name for the town of Placentia (47.2°N, 53.9°W). A few centuries ago fish was as important to the world economy as oil is today, and Plaisance was a bustling crossroads of the fish business, full of comings and goings.

Indigenous people were there seasonally for uncounted generations. Basques are known to have made the annual fishing voyage by at least the 16th century, perhaps earlier. Later when the place teemed with seasonal workers from Europe, a town grew up, lying low on the flat land around the harbour. Placentia is surrounded by steep, high hills and is overshadowed by the ruins of Fort Plaisance. The aura of the past hangs always in the air.

The rich fishery at Plaisance was well worth fighting over. The English and French squabbled viciously over the wealth of the seas around Newfoundland for centuries. In Placentia it ended only when the Treaty of Utrecht gave fishing rights to the English.

MATERIALS

125 metres light worsted weight wool (Group 3) in Dark (D). 125 metres light worsted weight wool (Group 3) in Light (L). Oddments of L may be sufficient for contrast colours. Samples were knit in Briggs and Little Regal 100% wool. Ring markers. 1 set of 4.00 mm double pointed needles.

SIZE

Ladies' Medium. Circumference: 9 inches (23 cm). Length: 11 inches (28 cm) from cast on to tip of middle finger. Thumb: 2.25 inches (6 cm). Index finger: 2.75 inches (7 cm). Middle finger: 3 inches (8 cm). Ring Finger: 2.75 inches (7 cm). Baby finger: 2.25 inches (6 cm). Length of thumb and fingers is adjustable.

GAUGE

24 stitches and 28 rows = 4 inches (10 cm).

SALT AND PEPPER PATTERN (S&P)

Worked over an odd number of stitches.

Round 1. (K1 with D, K1 with L). Repeat to end of round.

Round 2. (K1L, K1D). Repeat to end of round.

PLAISANCE CHART (25 stitches x 25 rounds)

How to Follow the Plaisance Chart. Change the shade of L on Rounds 3 and 6 if desired. Work Rounds 1–7 once. Work Rounds 2–7 three times more.

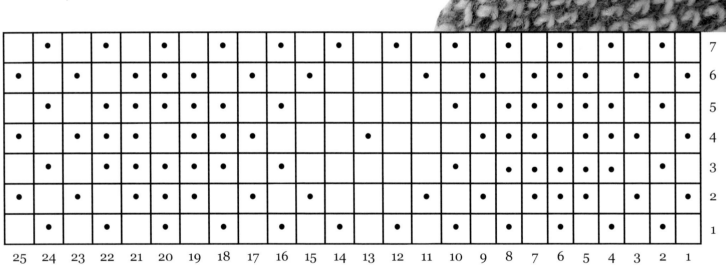

PLAISANCE THUMB GUSSET CHART

- K1D   Empty square = K1L

→ Make 1 Right with D   ← Make 1 Left with D

⇦ Make 1 Left with L   ⇨ Make 1 Right with L

Work charts from right to left, bottom to top. Always carry D on the left and L on the right to prevent streaks in the work. Instructions are for both hands unless otherwise indicated.

Wrist. Substitute a rib and 27 round stripe pattern of your choice if desired. To work tidy jogless stripes on the wrist as shown, with Dark (D) or the colour of your choice, cast on 36 stitches and join in a round, being careful not to twist.

First Stripe. Work 8 rounds in (K2, P1) ribbing. Break yarn.

Second Stripe. Next Round. Join Light (L) and knit this round with no purl stitches. **Next Round.** Slip the first stitch of the new colour purlwise to the last needle without working it, thereby shifting the beginning of the round one stitch to the left. K1, P1, (K2, P1) to last stitch, K1. Rib 7 more rounds as set. Break yarn.

Third Stripe. Join D and knit this round with no purl stitches. **Next Round.** Slip the first stitch of the new colour purlwise to the last needle without working it, thereby shifting the beginning of the round one stitch to the left. Rib to end of round. Work 6 rounds more ribbing in this colour.

Increase for Hand. With D, knit 1 round, increasing 13 stitches evenly spaced (49 stitches). Arrange stitches 25, 12, 12.

Round 1. Right Hand. Front. Join L and keeping D ahead (i.e., on the left) throughout, work Round 1 of Plaisance chart. These 25 stitches form the front of the mitten. **Palm.** K1D, K1L place marker. Work Round 1 of Plaisance thumb gusset chart. Place marker. (K1L, K1D) to end of round. These stitches form the palm. **Left Hand. Front.** Join L and, keeping D ahead (i.e., on the left) throughout, work Round 1 of Plaisance chart. These 25 stitches form the front of the mitten. **Palm.** (K1D, K1L) until 2 stitches remain in round. Place marker. Work Round 1 of Plaisance thumb gusset chart. Place marker. K1L.

PLAISANCE

They sailed a silken sea road to Plaisance.
The name rolls and curls like the silver wave licking the black, monumental shore.
Beyond this, a bastion of forest primeval.

Plaisance. A place of work.
A beach of pebbles inlaid between headlands.
Nowhere to go but out, out, out.

A place of soldiers, huddled in a cold stone fortress.
Waiting for the challenge.

A place of hard deaths and stony graves.
Exotic names etched on rocks for markers.

A place many called home long before we knew it.
And yet we feel it was always ours.

—Shirley A. Scott

Plaisance Gloves, Rosa Rugosa.

Both Hands. This sets up the Plaisance pattern on the front, salt and pepper (S&P) on the palm, and places the point of the thumb gusset with its two D outline stitches between the markers.

Round 2. Front. Work Round 2 of Plaisance chart. **Palm.** Work in S&P to marker. Slip marker. Work Round 2 of thumb gusset chart to marker. Slip marker. Work last stitch in S&P.

Continue working successive rounds of Plaisance on the front of the mitten, S&P on the palm and the thumb gusset within the markers until gusset Round 14 is complete, finishing the round in S&P (15 gusset stitches between markers). **Next Round.** Work in patterns as established to marker. Remove marker. Place 15 gusset stitches on a holder. Remove marker. Make 1 with correct S&P colour to bridge gap. Work in pattern to end of round (49 stitches).

Continue working Plaisance on the front and S&P on the palm until 25 rounds of Plaisance are complete. Finish the palm in S&P.

Next Round. Work 1 round of S&P on all stitches (49 stitches). Add more rounds of S&P here if extra length is needed to reach fingers. Cut lengths of waste yarn to hold finger stitches.

Divide for Fingers. Right Hand. Break yarns. **Front.** With Plaisance facing, and beginning at the right edge of the glove, put 6 stitches on holder for baby finger. Put next 6 stitches on holder for ring finger. Put next 7 stitches on holder for middle finger. **Palm.** Put corresponding 6 stitches on holder for baby finger, 6 stitches for ring finger, 6 stitches for middle finger. 12 stitches remain on needles for index finger.

Divide for Fingers. Left Hand. Front. With Plaisance facing, and beginning at the left edge of the glove, place 6 stitches on holder for baby finger. Put next 6 stitches on holder for ring finger. Place next 7 stitches on holder for middle finger. **Palm.** Place corresponding 6 stitches of palm on holder for baby finger. 6 stitches for ring finger. 6 stitches for middle finger. 12 stitches remain on needles for index finger.

Nan AT YOUR Side

When rejoining yarns and beginning each finger, leave long tails for darning ends and closing holes on the wrong side of the work.

〰〰〰

It's easier to distribute the stitches of glove fingers on three needles after you have worked a few rounds.

Right Index Finger. With Plaisance facing, rejoin yarns. Work 12 stitches in S&P. Cast on 7 stitches in correct S&P sequence (19 stitches). Divide work on 3 needles and join in a round. Note beginning of round. Work 15 rounds more of S&P, or until work reaches the tip of the finger. Work Finger Decrease Rounds 1 and 2.

Right Middle Finger. Transfer 7 stitches from front and 6 from palm to double pointed needles. With Plaisance facing,

rejoin yarns and work stitches of front in S&P. Pick up and knit 4 stitches in correct colour order from the base of the index finger. Work palm stitches in S&P. Cast on 2 stitches in correct S&P order (19 stitches). Divide work on 3 needles and join in a round. Note beginning of round. Work 17 rounds more in S&P, or until work reaches the tip of the finger. Work Finger Decrease Rounds 1 and 2.

Right Ring Finger. Transfer 6 stitches from front and 6 from palm to double pointed needles. With Plaisance facing, rejoin yarns and work front stitches in S&P. Pick up and knit 3 stitches in correct colour order from the base of the middle finger. Work palm stitches in S&P. Cast on 4 stitches in correct S&P order (19 stitches). Divide work on 3 needles and join in a round. Note beginning of round. Work 15 rounds more in S&P, or until work reaches the tip of the finger. Work Finger Decrease Rounds 1 and 2.

Right Baby Finger. Transfer 6 stitches from front and 6 from palm to double pointed needles. With Plaisance facing, rejoin yarns and work front stitches in S&P. Pick up and knit 5 stitches in correct colour order from the base of the ring finger. Work palm stitches in S&P (17 stitches). Divide work on 3 needles and join in a round. Note beginning of round. Work 12 rounds more in S&P, or until work reaches the tip of the finger. Work Finger Decrease Rounds 1 and 2.

Left Index Finger. With Plaisance facing, work 6 front stitches in S&P. Cast on 7 stitches in correct S&P order. Work 6 palm stitches in S&P (19 stitches). Divide work on 3 needles, join in a round, and note beginning of round. Work 15 rounds more of S&P, or until work reaches the tip of the finger. Work Finger Decrease Rounds 1 and 2.

Left Middle Finger. Transfer 7 stitches from front and 6 from palm to double pointed needles. With Plaisance facing, rejoin yarns and work front stitches in S&P. Cast on 2 stitches in correct S&P order. Work 6 palm stitches in S&P. Pick up and knit 4 stitches in correct colour order from the base of the index finger (19 stitches). Divide work on 3 needles and join in a round. Note beginning of round. Work 17 rounds more in S&P, or until work reaches the tip of the finger. Work Finger Decrease Rounds 1 and 2.

Left Ring Finger. Transfer 6 stitches from front and 6 from palm to double pointed needles. With Plaisance facing, rejoin yarns and work front stitches in S&P. Cast on 4 stitches in correct S&P order. Work palm stitches in S&P. Pick up and

knit 3 stitches in correct colour order from the base of the middle finger (19 stitches). Divide work on 3 needles and join in a round. Note beginning of round. Work 15 rounds more in S&P, or until work reaches the tip of the finger. Work Finger Decrease Rounds 1 and 2.

Left Baby Finger. Transfer 6 stitches from front and 6 from palm to double pointed needles. With Plaisance facing, rejoin yarns and work front stitches in S&P. Work palm stitches in S&P. Pick up and knit 5 stitches in correct colour order from the base of the ring finger (17 stitches). Divide work on 3 needles and join in a round. Note beginning of round. Work 12 rounds more in S&P or until work reaches the tip of the finger. Work Finger Decrease Rounds 1 and 2.

Finger Decrease Round 1. (K1 with correct colour in the S&P sequence. SSK with next colour in the sequence. K1 in S&P). Repeat to end of round, working any leftover stitches in S&P. Adjacent stitches in the same colour will be eliminated in the next round. **Finger Decrease Round 2.** (K1 with correct S&P colour. SSK with next colour in the S&P sequence). Repeat to end of round, working any leftover stitches in S&P. Break yarns. Thread through remaining stitches and secure.

Thumb. Transfer thumb stitches from holder to 2 double pointed needles. Rejoin yarns and knit these stitches in S&P. With another needle pick up and knit 4 stitches in S&P at the base of the thumb (19 stitches). Note beginning of round. Work 12 rounds more in S&P. Work Finger Decrease Rounds 1 and 2.

Finishing. Darn ends securely. Press well, omitting ribbing.

LANDFALL
Watch Cap in Three Sizes

DEGREE OF DIFFICULTY: * EASY DOES IT

This warm and colourful unisex classic with sizes for all is a wonderful way to use up oddments of yarn. It may be made with a single colour, two colours, or as many as you choose. Knit in the round, it is completely jogless, stripe flowing smoothly into stripe.

Though watch caps are usually worn aboard ship, this design got its start in the kitchen. It was inspired by a vintage tea cozy seen often on Newfoundland teapots.

MATERIALS

125 metres light worsted weight wool (Group 3) as main colour. Oddments of contrast colours. Samples were knit in Briggs and Little Regal. One 4.00 mm circular needle 40 cm long. 1 set of 4.00 mm double pointed needles. Cap may be knit entirely on double pointed needles if desired. Ring markers.

SIZE

Circumference: Small. 119 inches (48 cm). Medium. 21 inches (53 cm). Large. 22.5 inches (57 cm). For custom sizes, add or subtract stitches in groups of 8 and adjust yarn quantities accordingly.

GAUGE

20 stitches = 4 inches (10 cm).

Instructions are for a two-colour hat, with size S given first. M and L follow. Work ribbed stripe colours as desired.

   With main colour cast on 88 (96, 104) stitches. Join in a circle, being careful not to twist. Place marker. Work 20 rounds (K2, P2) ribbing, or desired length.

Nan
AT YOUR
Side

Be sure to wind a large ball of one colour for the ribbing, because joining yarns invisibly in ribbing can be difficult.

Watch Cap, Streely Maid Wrister.

Turning Ridge. Round 1. Knit. **Round 2.** Purl. **Round 3.** Remove marker. With yarn in back, slip 1 stitch purlwise. Replace marker. Knit to end of round. **Round 4.** Purl. Do not break main colour. Carry it loosely up the inside of the work.

Ribbed Stripes. Round 1. Join contrasting colour and knit to end of round. **Round 2.** Remove marker. Slip 1 stitch purlwise. Replace marker. Work (K2, P2) rib to end. **Rounds**

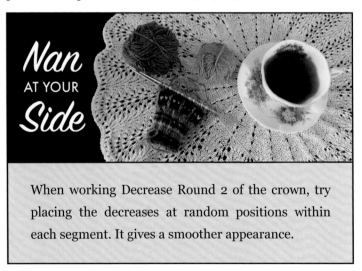

When working Decrease Round 2 of the crown, try placing the decreases at random positions within each segment. It gives a smoother appearance.

3–4. Work (K2, P2) rib to end. Break contrast colour if desired. **Round 5. Ridge.** With main colour, knit. **Round 6. Ridge.** Remove marker. Slip 1 stitch purlwise. Replace marker. Move yarn to front and purl to end of round.

Repeat these 6 rounds 5 times more, changing the contrast colour for each ridge and/or ribbed stripe if desired.

Shape Crown. Change to double pointed needles when work becomes tight. Divide the hat into 8 segments as follows. **Next Round.** K 11 (12, 13), place marker. Repeat to end of round. **Decrease Round 1.** Purl. **Decrease Round 2.** Knit until 2 stitches remain before marker, K2tog. Repeat to end of round (8 stitches decreased). Repeat these two rounds until 1 stitch remains in each segment (8 stitches). Purl 1 round. Break yarn, thread through remaining loops, pull tight, and secure ends.

Finishing. Press lightly on wrong side, omitting ribbing.

© Shirley A. Scott 2019

Watch Cap, Streely Maid Wrister, Witless Bay colours.

TUCKAMORE
His and Hers Trigger Mitts

DEGREE OF DIFFICULTY: ✳ ✳ TANGLY

Life is good when you live in a place with more trees than people. Many, many more. Much of the island of Newfoundland is covered with tuckamore, the stunted, weather-beaten little trees that sometimes grow densely as far as the eye can see. These hardy bushes embody the spirit of endurance that infuses life here. They are tough. They lean with the wind. They flourish in improbable places, clinging stubbornly to the edges of cliffs and thickly carpeting the barrens. They fight to live. They are hard to uproot.

The Tuckamore Trigger Mitt was first glimpsed on the hands of a mummer in a St. John's annual Mummers Parade. We took it from there.

MATERIALS

HIS. 2 shades of light worsted weight wool (Group 3), 125 metres Dark (D), 125 metres Light (L).

HERS. 2 shades of light worsted weight wool (Group 3), 125

Tuckamore leaning away from sea wind.

metres Dark (D), 125 metres Light (L). Samples were knit in Briggs and Little Regal. 1 set of 4.00 mm double pointed needles. 2 thinner double pointed needles for 3-needle bind off only (optional). Ring markers.

SIZE

HIS. Men's Large. Circumference: 10 inches (26 cm). Length of mitten from beginning of Tuckamore pattern: 8.5 inches (18 cm), or desired length. Trigger finger: 3.5 inches (9 cm), or desired length. Thumb: 2.75 inches (7 cm), or desired length. Length of hand, thumb, and trigger finger is adjustable.

HERS. Ladies' Medium. Circumference: 8 inches (21 cm). Length of mitten from beginning of Tuckamore pattern: 7 inches (18 cm), or desired length. Trigger finger: 3 inches (7.5 cm), or desired length. Thumb: 2.25 inches (5.5 cm), or desired length. Length of hand, thumb, and trigger finger is adjustable.

GAUGE

24 stitches and 28 rows = 4 inches (10 cm).

TUCKAMORE CHART

How to follow the Tuckamore Chart.

HIS. Horizontally. Work stitches 1–6 five times. Work stitch 7 once. Vertically. Work Rounds 1 and 2 once. Work Rounds 3–10 three times. Work Rounds 11, 12, 13 once (29 rounds).

HERS. Horizontally. Work stitches 1–6 four times. Work stitch 7 once. Vertically. Work Rounds 1 and 2 once. Work Rounds 3–10 twice. Work Rounds 11, 12, 13 once (21 rounds).

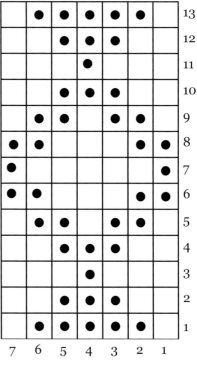

7	6	5	4	3	2	1	
	●	●	●	●	●		13
		●	●	●			12
			●				11
		●	●	●			10
	●	●		●	●		9
●	●				●	●	8
●						●	7
●	●				●	●	6
	●	●		●	●		5
		●	●	●			4
			●				3
		●	●	●			2
	●	●	●	●	●		1

HIS TUCKAMORE THUMB GUSSET CHART

HERS TUCKAMORE THUMB GUSSET CHART

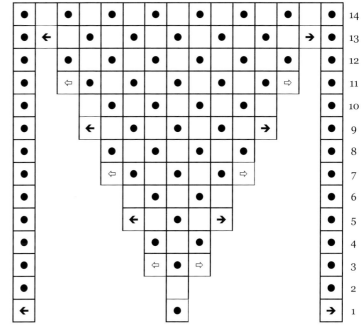

● K1D

→ Make 1 Right with D

⇦ Make 1 Left with L

Empty square = K1L

← Make 1 Left with D

⇨ Make 1 Right with L

SALT AND PEPPER PATTERN (S&P)

Worked over an odd number of stitches.

Round 1. (K1 with D, K1 with L). Repeat to end of round.

Round 2. (K1L, K1D). Repeat to end of round.

Instructions are for both hands and both sizes unless otherwise indicated. Instructions for HIS mittens are first. HERS follow, where necessary.

Work charts from right to left, bottom to top. Always carry D on the left and L on the right to prevent streaks in the work.

Wrist. With D cast on 42 (36) stitches. Join in a circle, being careful not to twist. Work 27 (24) rounds in (K2, P1) ribbing, or desired length, in a striped pattern of your choice.

Next Round. Knit, increasing 17 (13) stitches evenly spaced (59, 49 stitches). Arrange stitches (31, 14, 14) (25, 12, 12). Read **How to Follow the Tuckamore Chart.**

Round 1. Front. Join L and work Round 1 of the Tuckamore chart as directed on 31 (25) stitches for the front of the mitten.

Palm. Right Hand. Knit 1 with D, knit 1 with L. Place marker. Make 1 right leaning stitch with D. Knit 1 with D. Make 1 left leaning stitch with D. Place marker. Work (K1L, K1D) to end of round. There will be 3 D stitches between markers. **Palm. Left Hand.** (K1D, K1L) until 4 stitches remain in round. Place marker. M1R with D. K1D. M1L with D. Place marker. K1L, K1D, K1L. There will be 3 D stitches between markers.

Both Hands. This sets up the Tuckamore pattern on the front of the mitten and S&P on the palm, with the thumb gusset stitches between markers. The gusset is outlined with D stitches inside the markers.

Round 2. Front. Work Round 2 of Tuckamore as directed. **Palm.** Work S&P to marker. Slip marker. Work Round 2 of correct thumb gusset chart to next marker. Slip marker. Work S&P to end of round.

Continue in patterns as established working successive rounds of correct thumb gusset chart between markers on the palm until chart is complete, finishing the round in S&P. There will be 19 (15) gusset stitches between markers.

Next Round. Front. Work next round of Tuckamore on front. **Palm.** Work S&P to marker. Remove marker. Place gusset stitches on a holder. Cast on 1 stitch with correct colour in the sequence to bridge the gap. Remove marker. Work S&P to end of round (59, 49 stitches). **Next Round.** Work next round of Tuckamore on front, S&P on palm.

Continue working successive rounds of Tuckamore as directed on the front of the mitten and S&P on the palm until Tuckamore is complete, finishing the round in S&P.

With Tuckamore facing and beginning with K1D, work one round of S&P on all stitches. **HERS Only.** Work 3 rounds more in S&P.

TUCKAMORE

Small stunted evergreen tree with gnarled spreading roots, forming closely matted ground-cover on the barrens; low stunted vegetation; scrub.

~~~~~~~~~~

"Travelling alongshore between Bonne Bay and Cow Head, I sometimes used the sloping surface of tuckamore as a couch to rest upon."

~~~~~~~~~~

"We proceeded as usual to the Witless Bay Line ... and from thence some 13 miles on foot in over the tuckamores."

—*DICTIONARY OF NEWFOUNDLAND ENGLISH*

Reserve Trigger Finger. Use lengths of waste yarn for stitch holders. **Right Hand.** With Tuckamore facing, work 22 (17) stitches in S&P. Place next 9 (8) stitches of front on holder for trigger finger. Place corresponding 9 (8) stitches of palm on holder for trigger finger. Cast on 2 stitches in correct S&P order to bridge gap. Work S&P to end of round (43, 35 stitches).

Left Hand. Break yarns. Place first 9 (8) stitches of Tuckamore on holder for trigger finger. Place the corresponding 9 (8) stitches of palm on holder for trigger finger. With Tuckamore facing, rejoin yarns and work S&P on front, S&P on palm. Cast on 2 stitches in S&P to bridge gap (43, 35 stitches).

Both Hands. Work (15, 12) rounds more in S&P or until work reaches the tip of the little finger, ending with Tuckamore facing for next round. Arrange stitches (21, 11, 11) (17, 9, 9).

Shape Top. Note that some shaping rounds produce two adjacent stitches in the same colour at 4 points in the round. These will be eliminated in the following round.

Shaping Round 1. Front. K1 with correct S&P colour. SSK with next colour in the sequence. Work S&P until 3 stitches remain on front needle. K2tog with the same colour as the stitch just made. K1 in correct colour of S&P. **Palm.** Work as for front (4 stitches decreased).

Shaping Round 2. Front. K1 in S&P. SSK with next colour in the sequence. S&P to last 3 stitches of front. K2tog with next colour in the sequence. K1 in S&P. **Palm.** Work as for front (4 stitches decreased.)

Shaping Round 3. Work in S&P without decreasing. Repeat shaping rounds 1–3 (**HIS.** Twice more) (**HERS.** Once more) (19, 19 stitches). Break yarns, leaving a 16-inch tail of one for bind off.

3-Needle Bind Off. The hand is finished with a 3-needle bind off on the wrong side of the work.

Place stitches of front on a length of waste yarn. Place stitches of palm on another length of yarn. Turn mitten inside

out to work bind off on the wrong side, using the long tail.

Return stitches on holders to 2 double pointed needles. Hold these needles parallel to one another, the needle with the larger number of stitches nearest you. With a third double pointed needle and the long tail, K1 from the holding needle nearest you. Then knit 1 stitch from this needle together with 1 stitch of the opposite colour from the back needle. 2 stitches now on the working needle. Pass first stitch on working needle over second stitch to cast it off. 1 stitch remains on working needle. Continue to knit together 1 stitch from front and back holding needles and slipping the first stitch over second stitch on the working needle to bind off. Repeat until 1 stitch remains on working needle. Fasten and secure.

Trigger Finger. Transfer front stitches to a double pointed needle. Transfer palm stitches to a double pointed needle.

Right Trigger Finger. With Tuckamore facing, rejoin yarns. Work stitches on front and palm in S&P. With another double pointed needle pick up and knit 5 (3) stitches in correct S&P sequence from the base of the hand (23, 19 stitches).

Left Trigger Finger. With Tuckamore facing, rejoin yarns. Beginning with K1L work stitches of front in S&P. Pick up and knit 5 (3) stitches in correct colour sequence from base of hand. Work palm stitches in S&P (23, 19 stitches).

Both Hands. Note beginning of round. Divide stitches on 3 double pointed needles and work 17 (12) rounds more of S&P, or until work reaches the tip of the index finger.

Finger Decrease Round 1. (K1 with correct colour in the S&P sequence, SSK with next colour in the sequence, K1 in S&P), repeat to end of round working any leftover stitches in S&P. Adjacent stitches in the same colour will be eliminated in the next round.

Finger Decrease Round 2. (K1 with correct S&P colour, SSK with next colour in the S&P sequence), repeat to end of round, working any remaining stitches in S&P. Break yarns. Thread through remaining stitches and secure.

Thumb. Transfer thumb stitches from holder to two double pointed needles. Rejoin yarns and knit these stitches in S&P. With another needle, pick up and knit 4 (4) stitches in S&P at the base of the thumb (23, 19 stitches). Note beginning of round. Work 15 (12) rounds more in S&P, or until work reaches the tip of the thumb. Work Finger Decrease Rounds 1–2.

Finishing. Darn ends securely. Press lightly, omitting ribbing.

© Shirley A. Scott 2019

HELMET
Three Ways

DEGREE OF DIFFICULTY: ✳ ✳ TANGLY

Medieval soldiers wore helmets forged from steel and ornamented with silver. History tells us that the Vikings, led by Leif Eriksson, were the first explorers from Europe to land on Newfoundland's shores, in about 1000 CE. Archaeological evidence supporting this was discovered in the 1960s in a little-known place in Newfoundland called L'Anse aux Meadows (51.35°N, 55.53°W). On the northernmost tip of the Great Northern Peninsula, it is now designated a UNESCO World Heritage Site and is the only authenticated Norse site in North America. There is now a recreated Viking settlement there.

The Icelandic sagas mention the place name Vinland. Some believe the Vikings gave this name to the island of Newfoundland. Others believe Vinland was a much larger region of eastern North America.

Unlike those heavy metal helmets of old, this versatile helmet design, inspired by both medieval soldiers and Vikings, is warm and cozy. It is meant to help you battle the elements, not the enemy. Wear it three ways. The backflap warms your neck when the wind is at your back. Turn it up in milder weather, then turn it around to cover your forehead when the icy wind hits face on.

SIZE

Small. Circumference: 19–20 inches (48–50 cm).

Medium–Large. Circumference: 22–23 inches (56–58 cm).

MATERIALS

Small. 250 metres light worsted weight wool (Group 3). 1 set double pointed needles size 3.25 mm, 10 inches (26 cm) long. 1 set double pointed needles 3.75, 10 inches (26 cm) long. Sample knit using Briggs and Little Regal 100% wool.

Medium–Large. 200 metres medium worsted weight wool (Group 4). 1 set 3.50 mm double pointed needles, 10 inches (26 cm) long. 1 set 4.00 mm double pointed needles, 10 inches (26 cm) long. Sample knit with Briggs and Little Heritage 100% wool.

Both sizes. Stitch markers. Sharp darning needle.

GAUGE

10 stitches = 2 inches (5 cm) worked in stocking stitch using light worsted weight (Group 3) and 3.75 mm needles.

9 stitches = 2 inches (5 cm) worked in stocking stitch using medium worsted weight (Group 4) and 4.00 mm needles.

Back Flap. Knit flat. Using smaller needles for the size selected, cast on 53 stitches. Working back and forth on just 2 needles work as follows. **Row 1.** (K1, P1). Repeat to last stitch, K1. **Row 2.** As Row 1. This establishes the moss stitch pattern. Repeat these 2 rows until the back flap measures 2.5 inches (6.5 cm).

Using another needle, cast on 40 stitches for front of cap. Place the marker for beginning of round. Join in a round, being careful not to twist. Keeping continuity of the moss stitch pattern, work 9 rounds moss stitch around the circumference.

Next Round. Continue in moss stitch, increasing 3 stitches evenly spaced on needle 1. Increase 2 stitches evenly spaced on needle 2. Increase 2 stitches evenly spaced on needle 3, the front of the cap (100 stitches).

Change to the larger needles. Arrange stitches as follows. Needle 1. 29 stitches. Needle 2. 29 stitches. Needle 3. 42 stitches (front of the cap).

Set up Stocking Stitch and Moss Stitch Panels. In Round 1 the moss stitch sequence is disrupted in more than one place. It is restored in Round 2.

Moss Stitch Panel (5 stitches)

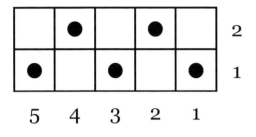

● = Purl   Empty square = Knit

Round 1. Slip marker. K14. Moss Panel Round 1. Place marker. (K20, Moss Round 1. Place marker). Repeat (to) 2 more times. K6.

Round 2. K14. Moss Panel Round 2. Slip marker. (K20, Moss Panel Round 2). Slip marker. Repeat (to) 2 times more. K6.

Pattern is now set with stocking stitch panels flanked on either side by moss stitch panels, the centre panel is lined up in the middle of the front of the cap. Continue in established patterns until the work measures 4.25 inches (Medium–Large 4.75 inches) when measured from cast on edge at the front, ending with Moss Panel Round 2.

The name L'Anse aux Meadows is thought by some to be a corruption of the French words L'Anse aux Méduses, or Jellyfish Cove. Another more poetic interpretation is "the bay with meadows."

Agnes Walsh was named poet laureate for St. John's in 2006, the first to hold the position.

Out of the rustling of tall grass
onto an upshoot of boulder and sparse fir
came the trampling of a gang of small boys.
Armed with stick guns and swords
and armed better still with whoops and shrills
they advanced and gained on the sheep.

—AGNES WALSH, "OUT OF THE RUSTLING OF TALL GRASS"

Shape Top. Remove beginning marker. K4. Replace beginning marker. Remove sectional markers when you come to them.

Round 1. Decrease Round. K8, K2tog, (Moss Panel Round 1, K2tog, K16, K2tog). Repeat from (to) 2 times more. Moss Panel Round 1, K2tog, K8.

Round 2. K9, (Moss Panel Round 2, K18). Repeat from (to) 2 times more. Moss Panel Round 2, K9.

Round 3. Decrease Round. K7, K2tog, (Moss Panel Round 1, K2tog, K14, K2tog). Repeat from (to) 2 times more. Moss Panel Round 1, K2tog, K7.

Round 4. K8, (Moss Panel Round 2, K16). Repeat from (to) 2 times more. Moss Panel Round 2, K8.

Round 5. Decrease Round. K6, K2tog, (Moss Panel Round 1, K2tog, K12, K2tog), repeat from (to) 2 times more. Moss Panel Round 1, K2tog, K6.

Round 6. K7, (Moss Panel Round 2, K14). Repeat from (to) 2 times more. Moss Panel Round 2, K7.

Continue decreasing in this manner on alternate rounds until 36 stitches remain, ending with a round with no decreases.

Complete Top. Round 1. K2tog, (P1, K3tog, P1, K2tog, K2tog). Repeat from (to) to last 7 stitches. P1, K3tog, P1, K2tog.

Round 2. K2, P1, (K4, P1). Repeat from (to) to last 2 stitches. K2.

Round 3. K2tog, (K1, K2tog, K2tog). Repeat from (to) to last 2 stitches. K2tog.

Next Round. Knit. Break yarn, leaving an 8-inch (20 cm) tail. Thread though remaining stitches, draw up, and fasten securely.

Finishing. Darn any remaining ends, turn inside out and gently press, omitting the moss stitch portions.

© Christine LeGrow 2019

Helmet, Streely Maid Wrister.

STAR OF LOGY BAY CAP

DEGREE OF DIFFICULTY: ✶✶ TANGLY

Logy Bay (47.64°N, 52.69°W) appears on a map of the area as early as 1675. In 1818 a fisherman named Luke Ryan built a fishing room there and it was a fishing settlement until the mid-20th century. Today it is home to the Ocean Sciences Centre and the Dr. Joe Brown Aquatic Research building, Memorial University of Newfoundland. These cold ocean research laboratories are leaders in studying the North Atlantic fishery and related oceanography.

FISHING ROOM

A tract or a parcel of land on the waterfront of a cove or harbour from which a fishery is conducted; the stores, sheds, "flakes," wharves and other facilities where the catch is landed and processed, and the crew housed.

—DICTIONARY OF NEWFOUNDLAND ENGLISH

The many stars visible in the sky over the ocean at Logy Bay inspired this cap. In a famous song by the same name, the star is actually a lovely young maid that has captured a sailor's heart. And as the lyrics say, may heaven above send down its love on the star of Logy Bay.

SIZE

Adult Medium. Circumference: 21–22 inches (53–56 cm).

MATERIALS

Medium worsted weight yarn (Group 4). To knit as shown three colours are required: 70 metres main colour, 70 metres light contrast colour, 70 metres dark contrast colour. Samples were knit with Briggs and Little Heritage 100% wool. 1 set 3.50 mm double pointed needles. 1 set 4.50 mm double pointed needles. 5 place markers. Sharp darning needle.

GAUGE

15 stitches = 3 inches (7.5 cm) on 4.50 mm needles.

STAR OF LOGY BAY CAP CHART

How to Follow the Star of Logy Bay Cap Chart. Work chart from right to left and bottom to top. Join L at start of Round 1 of chart. Join D at start of Round 2 of chart. Break D at end of Round 19. Break L at end of Round 20.

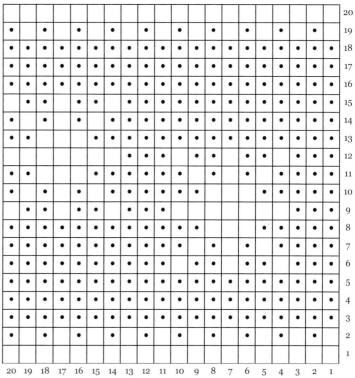

• K1D   Empty square = K1L

Using 3.50 mm needles and main shade, cast on 93 stitches. Join in a round, being careful not to twist.

Band. Round 1. (K1, P1). Repeat to last stitch. K1. **Round 2.** (P1, K1). Repeat to last stitch. P1. These two rounds set up the moss stitch pattern. Repeat them 4 times more. **Round 11.** Maintaining moss stitch pattern, increase 7 stitches evenly spaced.

Change to 4.50 mm needles and work 4 rounds stocking stitch. Break main colour.

Cap. Work Round 1 of the chart 5 times, placing a marker after each completion (100 stitches). Continue each round in this manner, slipping the markers as you come to them, until 20 rounds of the chart are complete.

Rejoin main colour and work 2 rounds stocking stitch, removing all but beginning of round marker on last round.

Shape Top. Round 1. (K8, K2tog). Repeat to end of round. **Round 2.** Knit. **Round 3.** (K7, K2tog). Repeat to end of round. **Round 4.** Knit.

Continue decreasing in this manner, having 1 stitch fewer between the decreases on alternate rounds until the (K1, K2tog) round is complete. **Next Round.** (K2tog) to end of round. Draw up and fasten securely.

Finishing. Turn cap inside out. Darn in the ends and trim neatly. Gently press, omitting the band.

© Christine LeGrow 2019

A mauzy day in Logy Bay.

STAR OF LOGY BAY
Trigger Mitts for Young Adults

DEGREE OF DIFFICULTY: ✳ ✳ TANGLY

The North Star is highly visible from Logy Bay at certain times of the year. It has guided mariners home for centuries. In her 1859 book, Newfoundlander Isabella Whiteford refers to such stars in one poem.

> *I have seen the mariner tempest-toss'd*
> *Afar from the trackless deep,*
> *And I was his guide when all hope was lost,*
> *When the friends he loved were asleep.*
> *I have marked the starting tear,*
> *As his eye was turned on me.*
> *He knew that a friend was near*
> *On the dark and trackless sea.*

> –Isabella Whiteford, "The Polar Star"

SIZE

Adult Medium. Circumference: 9.25 inches (23.5 cm). Length from beginning of the Star of Logy Bay motif to cast off 6.75 inches (17 cm).

MATERIALS

Medium worsted weight wool (Group 4).

Two-colour version. 100 metres Dark (D), 100 metres Light (L).

Three-colour version. 100 metres Dark (D), 100 metres Light (L), 75 metres of an additional Contrast colour. 1 set 3.25 mm double pointed needles. 1 set 3.50 mm double pointed needles. Ring markers, sharp darning needle, stitch holders.

GAUGE

9 stitches = 2 inches (5 cm), using 3.50 mm needles.

SALT AND PEPPER PATTERN (S&P)

Worked on an odd number of stitches.

Round 1. (K1D, K1L). Repeat to end of round.
Round 2. (K1L, K1D). Repeat to end of round.

STAR OF LOGY BAY TRIGGER MITT CHART (SLB)

How to Follow the Star of Logy Bay Trigger Mitt Chart.
The Star of Logy Bay Trigger Mitt can be knit using two or three colours. Plan your colour scheme before beginning. The colours are named Dark, Light, and Contrast. If using three colours, empty squares = Light and ● = Contrast. Break and join Dark and Contrast at the beginning and end of the chart.

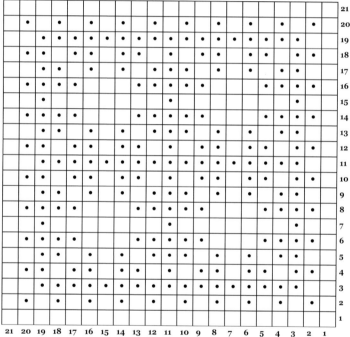

● Dark in the two-colour option. Contrast in the three-colour option.

Empty square = Light

STAR OF LOGY BAY THUMB GUSSET CHART

● K1D   Empty square = K1L

⇨ Make 1 Right with L   ⇦ Make 1 Left with L

Work charts from right to left, bottom to top. Always carry D on the left and L on the right to prevent colour streaks in the work. When Contrast replaces D in the three-colour version, carry Contrast on the left. Instructions are for both hands, unless otherwise indicated. Read instructions before casting on.

Both Hands. Wrist. With D cast on 39 stitches. Join in round being careful not to twist. Work (K2, P1) ribbing in your choice of solid colour or stripes until ribbing measures 3 inches (7.5 cm), increasing 8 stitches evenly spaced on final round. Break yarn. Arrange stitches as follows. Needle 1: 21 stitches (front of mitten). Needle 2: 13 stitches. Needle 3: 13 stitches.

Right Hand. Set Up Round. Change to 3.50 mm needles. Join and break colours throughout as described above. **Round 1.** Work Star of Logy Bay (SLB) chart. Place marker. Work Round 1 of thumb gusset chart. Place marker. Work Round 1 of S&P pattern to end of round. The SLB chart is now positioned on the front of the mitten, the thumb gusset follows between the markers, and the S&P pattern is established on the palm. **Round 2.** Work Round 2 of SLB chart, Round 2 of thumb gusset chart (increase round), Round 2 of S&P pattern to end of round.

Whiteford poems.

Continue working successive rounds of SLB on the front and thumb gusset and S&P on the palm until Round 12 is complete. There are 11 thumb gusset stitches between the 2 outline stitches.

Round 13. Work Round 13 of SLB on the front of the mitten. Remove marker. Slip the 13 stitches of the thumb gusset, including the 2 outline stitches, to a holding thread. Cast on 5 stitches in correct colour sequence to bridge the gap. Remove marker. Work S&P pattern to the end of the round. There are 21 stitches on needle 1 (front of the mitten). Needles 2 and 3 share the 26 palm stitches. The thumb gusset is now complete. Continue to work SLB chart on the front and S&P on the palm until Round 21 is complete.

Reserve Right Index Finger Stitches. Slip 2 stitches from the beginning of needle 2 to needle 1 for the front of the mitten (23 stitches on needle 1). Place the last 7 stitches of needle 1 and the first 7 stitches of needle 2 on a holder. These stitches will become part of the first round of the index finger.

Complete Right Hand. Round 22. With SLB facing, join yarns. Keeping S&P colour sequence correct work S&P on the front of the mitten. Cast on 4 stitches in S&P to bridge the gap. Work S&P to end of round. Work 13 rounds more or desired length in S&P.

Set Up Top Shaping. Slip 2 stitches from the beginning of needle 2 to the end of needle 1. Arrange stitches as follows. Needle 1: 18 stitches (front of the mitten). Needle 2: 10 stitches. Needle 3: 9 stitches.

Shape Top. On odd-numbered rounds, decreasing will create two adjacent stitches of the same colour. On the following even-numbered rounds, these stitches will be worked together, restoring the correct colour sequence. Decreases are made one stitch in from the edge at four points in the round.

Shaping Round 1. Needle 1. K1 in correct colour. SSK with the next colour in the sequence. Resume S&P pattern on the next stitch, having made 2 adjacent stitches of the same colour. Work in pattern until 3 stitches remain on the needle. K2tog in the same colour as the stitch just made. Work the last stitch in the correct colour. Needle 2. K1, SSK as above, work in pattern to end of the needle. Needle 3. Work in pattern until 3 stitches remain before the end of the needle. K2tog in the same colour as the stitch just made. K1 in correct colour.

Shaping Round 2. Work SSK and K2tog decreases in S&P at the same points as the previous round. Colour sequence will be restored. Decrease in this manner until 13 stitches remain. Proceed to 3-Needle Bind Off.

3-Needle Bind Off. Place the stitches from the front of the mitten on a length of waste yarn. Place the stitches of the palm on another length of yarn. Turn the mitten inside out to work the bind off. Return the stitches from the holders to two thinner double pointed needles for convenience. Hold these needles parallel to one another. Have the needle with the greater number of stitches nearest you. With a third

needle and using the long tail of D, K1 from the holding needle nearest you. Then knit 1 stitch from the front needle together with 1 stitch of the opposite colour from the back needle. 2 stitches now on the working needle. Pass first stitch on the working needle over the second stitch to cast it off. 1 stitch remains on the working needle. Continue to knit together 1 stitch from the front and back holding needles and slipping the first stitch over the second stitch on the working needle to cast off. Repeat until 1 stitch remains. Thread through remaining stitch. Draw up and fasten securely.

Right Index Finger. With SLB facing, slip first 7 stitches from the holder onto needle 1. Slip next 7 stitches onto a second needle. Join yarns and keeping S&P correct, knit 7 stitches on needle 1, 7 stitches on needle 2. With needle 3, pick up and knit 5 stitches at the base of the finger in the correct colour sequence (19 stitches).

Work 15 rounds in S&P pattern, or desired length. Work Finger Decrease Rounds 1 and 2.

Finger Decrease Round 1. (K1 with correct S&P colour. SSK with next colour in the sequence. K1 in S&P.) Repeat to end of round, knitting any leftover stitches in S&P.

Finger Decrease Round 2. (K1, SSK) in S&P to end of round, working any remaining stitches in S&P. Break yarns, thread though remaining stitches, draw up, and fasten securely.

Right Thumb. Transfer 13 gusset stitches onto 2 needles. With SLB facing rejoin yarns, working 1 D stitch over D stitch then resuming S&P throughout the round. Pick up 6 stitches at the base of the thumb (19 stitches). Work 11 rounds more, or desired length, in S&P pattern. Work Finger Decrease Rounds 1 and 2.

Left Hand. Set Up Round. Round 1. Join yarns and work SLB chart on needle 1 for the front of the mitten. Work Round 1 of S&P pattern until 5 stitches remain in the round. Place marker. Work Round 1 of the thumb gusset chart. Place marker. The thumb gusset is now in position for the left hand.

Logy Bay story.

Round 2. Work Round 2 of SLB chart, Round 2 in S&P pattern on the palm. Slip marker. Work Round 2 of thumb gusset chart (increase round). Slip marker.

Continue working successive rounds of SLB on the front of the mitten, S&P on the palm and thumb gusset chart until Round 12 is complete. There are 11 thumb gusset stitches between the 2 outline stitches.

Round 13. Work Round 13 of SLB chart. Work S&P to marker. Remove marker. Slip 13 thumb gusset stitches onto a holder. Cast on 5 stitches in correct colour sequence to bridge the gap. Remove marker. The left thumb gusset is now complete (47 stitches).

Beginning with Round 14, continue working SLB on front and S&P on the palm until Round 21 is complete. Break yarns.

Reserve Left Index Finger Stitches. Slip 2 stitches from end of needle 3 onto the beginning of needle 1 (23 stitches on needle 1). Slip last 7 stitches from needle 3 and the first 7 stitches of needle 1 onto waste yarn for the index finger.

Complete Left Hand. With SLB facing, rejoin yarns. Work S&P pattern on front and palm of the mitten, casting on 4 stitches in correct colour sequence to bridge the gap. Work 13 rounds more or desired length in S&P. **Next Round.** Work S&P to last 2 stitches. Slip these 2 stitches to the beginning of needle 1 (front of the mitten). Arrange stitches as follows. Needle 1: 18 stitches. Needle 2: 10 stitches. Needle 3: 9 stitches.

Work Shape Top and 3-Needle Bind Off as for right hand.

Left Index Finger. With SLB facing, slip the 7 stitches from front holder to needle 1. Slip remaining 7 stitches from the thread onto another needle. With SLB facing, rejoin yarns at the right edge of the mitten and, keeping S&P pattern correct, work the 7 stitches of needle 1. With another needle, pick up and knit 5 stitches at the base of the finger in the correct colour sequence. Work remaining 7 stitches in S&P.

Work 15 rounds in S&P pattern or desired length. Work Finger Decrease Rounds 1 and 2.

Left Thumb. Transfer 13 gusset stitches onto 2 needles. With palm facing, rejoin yarns and complete in the same manner as right thumb.

Finishing. Carefully darn all ends, paying particular attention to the areas where yarns were broken and joined. Correct puckers and loose stitches as you darn. Trim darned ends neatly. Press gently under a damp cloth, omitting ribbing.

© Christine LeGrow 2019

NOGGIN COVE
CAP FOR ADULTS

DEGREE OF DIFFICULTY: ✳ ✳ TANGLY

Where exactly is Noggin Cove? It is just west of Carmanville, on the southern side of Hamilton Sound, of course (49.42°N, 54.32°W). What exactly is a sound? A large deep channel in the ocean between two pieces of land. Unless you are referring to a codfish, in which case a sound is part of the fish's body. Words have a lot of different uses in Newfoundland.

Noggin Cove is a very tiny town whose population has fluctuated between 6 and 258 from the mid-19th century to the present day. It shares its name with Noggin Cove Island, 5 kilometres out to sea. How did the island get its name? Nobody knows for sure. A noggin is a small cask that holds butter or rum. How tasty if the cask held both at the same time!

Noggins were also used for mixing horse feed. There are complex modern meanings for the word as well.

In Newfoundland we also refer to our heads as noggins, the inspiration for this cap. While the look is *faux* thrum, it is knit simply in fairisle and texture patterns. Thick, warm, and extra cozy, it will protect your noggin from the cold.

Don't fall and hit your noggin!
Words of caution for many a youngster.

Wikipedia explains noggin as a protein that is involved in the development of many body tissues, including nerve, muscles, and bone. In humans, noggin is encoded by the NOG gene.

"Every stitch bears the indelible mark of all craftspeople who came before. Every movement of the knitter's needle is moved and guided by history and by place."

—PAUL DOUCET, A CLOSE FAMILY FRIEND,
WAS USING HIS NOGGIN WHEN HE WROTE THIS.

SIZE

Circumference: 21–22 inches (53–56 cm).

MATERIALS

Main colour: 200 metres medium worsted weight wool (Group 4). Contrast colour: 20 metres (or an oddment) medium worsted weight wool (Group 4). Samples were knit with Briggs and Little Heritage 100% wool. 1 set of 3.50 mm double pointed needles. 1 set of 4.00 mm double pointed needles. Marker. Sharp finishing needle.

GAUGE

9 stitches = 2 inches (5 cm) on 4.00 mm needles in stocking stitch.

Noggin Cove, Double Band.

NOGGIN COVE CHART

8	7	6	5	4	3	2	1	
P						P		8
	P				P			7
		P		P				6
			P				▨	5
		P		P				4
	P				P			3
P						P		2
			▨				P	1

▨ = K1 with Contrast Colour   P = Purl 1

Empty Square = K1 Main Colour

For extra warmth follow instructions for Double Band. For less bulk make the traditional Single Band.

Using main shade and 3.50 mm double pointed needles cast on 92 stitches. Mark beginning of round. **Double Band. Round 1.** (K1, P1). Repeat to end of round. Repeat this round 10 times more. **Round 12.** Purl. Work 10 rounds in (K1, P1) ribbing. **Next Round.** Work in ribbing increasing 4 stitches evenly spaced (96 stitches).

Single Band. Work 10 rounds (K1, P1) ribbing. **Next Round.** Work in ribbing increasing 4 stitches evenly spaced (96 stitches).

Cap. Change to larger double pointed needles. **Round 1.** Join contrast colour and begin Noggin Cove Chart, repeating the pattern 12 times to end of round. Carry the contrast colour behind the main shade in Rounds 1 and 5. On rounds where contrast colour is not in use carry it loosely up the side of the work. When carrying the colour not in use horizontally for more than three stitches weave it through the back of the work to maintain elasticity.

Continue working successive rounds of Noggin Cove Chart until 32 rounds are complete. **Next Round.** Work Round 1. Break contrast colour.

Shape Top. Round 1. (K6, K2tog). Repeat to end of round. **Round 2.** Knit. **Round 3.** (K5, K2tog). Repeat to end of round. **Round 4.** Knit. Continue decreasing in this manner, having 1 stitch less between the decreases on alternate rounds until 12 stitches remain on the needle, ending with a knit round. Break yarn leaving a tail 8 inches (20 cm) long, thread through the remaining stitches. Draw up and fasten securely.

Finishing. Double Band Cap. Turn cap inside out. Using main colour yarn sew cast on edge to last round of ribbing, being careful not to pull tightly. Darn remaining ends. **Single Band Cap.** Darn ends.

© Christine LeGrow 2019

WESLEYVILLE
Trigger Mitts for Men

DEGREE OF DIFFICULTY ✳ ✳ TANGLY

Wesleyville (49.1°N, 53.6°W) and its nearby communities in Bonavista Bay are sacred ground to artist David Blackwood. His work renders the people, places, and dramatic events of not-so-long-ago Newfoundland in fine detail. The steadfast faces, beloved homes with their curtained windows, the tools in use, vessels at sea, islands, shores and capes, majestic icebergs, and whales all spring to life. Each image seems bathed in radiant light, conveying awe and respect for the hard, independent life by the sea. With impeccable attention to individual stitches, he also renders Newfoundland mittens in detail. This mitten pattern is offered as a tribute to David Blackwood and to his birthplace.

SIZE

Men's Medium. Length: 11.5 inches (29 cm) from cast on to mitten tip. Circumference: 9.5 inches (24 cm). Thumb: 3 inches (8 cm). Trigger finger: 3 inches (7.5 cm). Length of hand, thumb, and trigger finger is adjustable.

MATERIALS

1 set of 4.00 mm double pointed needles. 2 thinner double pointed needles for 3-needle bind off only (optional). 250 metres light worsted weight wool (Group 3) in Dark (D). 250 metres light worsted weight wool (Group 3) in Light (L). Ring markers. Samples were knit in Briggs and Little Regal. Lengths of yarn for stitch holders.

GAUGE

24 stitches and 28 rows = 4 inches (10 cm).

SALT AND PEPPER PATTERN (S&P)

Worked over an odd number of stitches.

Round 1. (K1 with D, K1 with L). Repeat to end of round, ending with D.
Round 2. (K1L, K1D). Repeat to end of round, ending with K1L.

David Blackwood , *Home from Bragg's Island.*

When we look at a David Blackwood print we look at a world where every object has life and history ... The detail of this world, the way a created object could stand for and tell us all about the owner of that object ... The design of diamonds with the little arrow shapes holds shades of windows, of paint that keeps the devil from a fishing shed; the way the fingers are planned show the way nets must be handled; the worn wood of the cutting table where the mitts are placed is vital; the way the mitts are arranged tells us about the person who placed them there ... Without ever having seen Uncle Sam we know about him and his life.

—WILLIAM GOUGH, IN *THE ART OF DAVID BLACKWOOD*

WESLEYVILLE CHART (14 stitches x 14 rows)

14	13	12	11	10	9	8	7	6	5	4	3	2	1	
	•		•		•		•		•		•		•	14
•		•	•	•		•		•				•		13
	•		•	•	•		•						•	12
•	•	•			•	•	•			•				11
	•		•	•	•		•						•	10
•		•	•	•		•		•				•		9
	•		•		•		•		•		•		•	8
•		•		•		•		•		•		•		7
	•				•		•		•	•	•		•	6
•					•		•	•	•	•	•			5
		•				•	•	•		•	•	•		4
•					•			•	•	•	•	•		3
	•				•		•	•	•	•	•		•	2
•		•		•		•		•		•		•		1

WESLEYVILLE THUMB GUSSET CHART

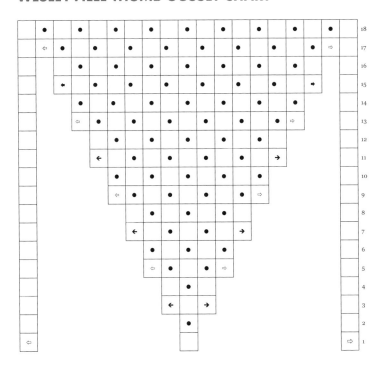

- ● K1D
- → Make 1 Right with D
- ⇨ Make 1 Right with L

Empty square = K1L
- ← Make 1 Left with D
- ⇦ Make 1 Left with L

Work charts from R to L, bottom to top. Always carry D on the left and L on the right to prevent streaks in work. Instructions apply to both hands, unless otherwise indicated.

Wrist. With D, cast on 42 stitches. Divide evenly on 3 needles and join in a circle, being careful not to twist. Work 27 rounds, or desired length, of (K2, P1) rib in a stripe pattern of your choice. **Next Round.** With D knit, increasing 15 stitches evenly spaced (57 stitches). Arrange work on needles: 28 stitches, 15 stitches, 14 stitches.

Round 1. Front. Join L and, keeping D ahead (i.e., on the left) throughout, work Round 1 of Wesleyville chart twice (28 stitches) for the front of the mitten. **Palm. Right Hand.** K1L, K1D. Place marker. Make 1 right leaning stitch with L, K1L, make 1 left leaning stitch with L. Place marker. (K1D, K1L) to end of round. There will be 3 L stitches between markers. **Palm. Left Hand.** (K1L, K1D) until 3 stitches remain in round. Place marker. Make 1 right leaning stitch with L, K1L. Make 1 left leaning stitch with L. Place marker. K1D, K1L. There are 3 L stitches between markers.

This sets up 28 Wesleyville pattern stitches on the front and S&P on the palm, with the thumb gusset between the markers. The thumb gusset is outlined in L stitches inside the markers.

Round 2. Front. Work Round 2 of Wesleyville chart twice. **Palm.** Work in S&P to marker. Slip marker. Work Round 2 of thumb gusset chart to next marker. Slip marker. Work in S&P to end of round.

Continue working successive rounds of Wesleyville on the front of the mitten, S&P on the palm, and the thumb gusset within the markers, until Round 18 of the thumb gusset is complete.

Next Round. Work in patterns as established to marker. Remove marker. Place gusset stitches on a holder. Remove next marker. Make 1 stitch with correct S&P colour to bridge gap. Work in pattern to end of round (57 stitches). Continue working Wesleyville on the front and S&P on the palm until Round 28 of Wesleyville is complete, finishing the palm in S&P.

Next Round. Work S&P to end of round. Add more rounds of S&P to increase length before trigger finger if desired.

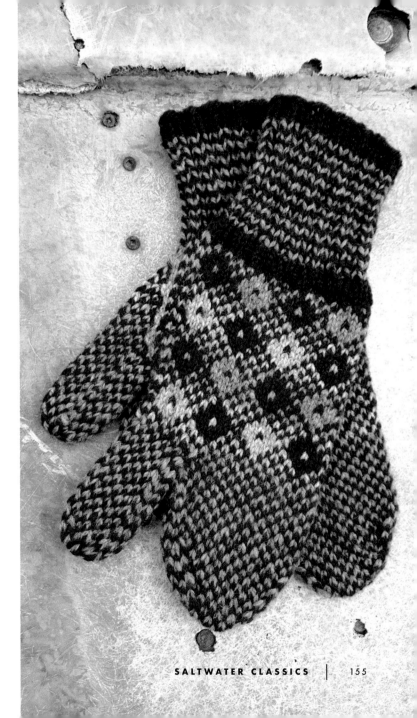

Reserve Trigger Finger Stitches. Right Hand. Work S&P on 20 stitches of front. Place next 16 stitches on holder for trigger finger. Cast on 2 stitches in correct S&P in order to bridge gap. Work S&P on palm to end of round (43 stitches).

Left Hand. Break yarns. At the same edge of the mitten as the thumb, place 8 stitches of front on holder for trigger finger. Place the corresponding 8 stitches of palm on holder for trigger finger. With Wesleyville facing, rejoin yarns and work S&P on front, S&P on palm. Cast on 2 stitches in S&P to bridge gap (43 stitches).

Both Hands. Work 13 rounds more in S&P, or until work reaches the tip of the little finger, ending with Wesleyville facing for next round. Arrange stitches 21, 11, 11.

Shape Top. Note that some shaping rounds produce two adjacent stitches in the same colour at 4 points in the round. These will be eliminated in the following round.

Shaping Round 1. Front. K1 with correct S&P colour. SSK with next colour in the sequence. Work S&P until 3 stitches remain on front needle. K2tog with the same colour as the stitch just made. K1 in correct colour of S&P. **Palm.** Work as for front (4 stitches decreased).

Shaping Round 2. Front. K1 in S&P. SSK with next colour in the sequence. S&P to last 3 stitches on front needle. K2tog with next colour in the sequence. K1 in S&P. **Palm.** Work as for front (4 stitches decreased.)

Shaping Round 3. Work in S&P without decreasing.

Repeat Shaping Rounds 1–3 two more times. Break yarns, leaving a long tail of one colour for bind off.

3-Needle Bind Off. The hand is finished with a 3-needle bind off on the wrong side of the work.

Place stitches of front on a length of waste yarn. Place stitches of palm on another length of yarn. Turn mitten inside out to work bind off on the wrong side, using the long tail.

Return stitches on holders to two thinner double pointed needles for easier working. Hold these needles parallel to one another, the needle with the greater number of stitches nearest you. With a third double pointed needle and long tail, K1 from the holding needle nearest you. Then knit 1 stitch from the front needle together with 1 stitch of the opposite colour from the back needle. There are now 2 stitches on the working needle. Pass first stitch on working needle over second stitch to cast it off. 1 stitch remains on working needle. Continue to knit together 1 stitch from front and back holding needles and slipping the first stitch over second stitch on the working needle to cast off. Repeat until 1 stitch remains. Fasten off and darn ends.

Trigger Finger. Transfer 8 stitches from front holder to a double pointed needle. Transfer 8 stitches from palm to a double pointed needle. **Right Trigger Finger.** With Wesleyville facing, rejoin yarns, and work 16 stitches in S&P. With another double pointed needle pick up and knit 5 stitches in correct S&P sequence from the base of the hand (21 stitches). **Left Trigger Finger.** With Wesleyville facing, rejoin yarns and work 8 stitches of front in S&P. Pick up and knit 5 stitches in correct colour sequence from base of hand. Work 8 stitches of palm in S&P (21 stitches). **Both Hands.** Note beginning of round. Arrange stitches on 3 needles and work 17 rounds more of S&P, or until work reaches the tip of the index finger.

Finger Decrease Round 1. (K1 with correct colour in the S&P sequence. SSK with next colour in the sequence. K1 in S&P). Repeat to end of round, working any leftover stitches in S&P. Adjacent stitches in the same colour will be eliminated in the next round. **Finger Decrease Round 2.** (K1 with correct S&P colour. SSK with next colour in the S&P sequence) to end of round, working any leftover stitches in S&P. Break yarns. Thread through remaining stitches and secure.

Thumb. Transfer thumb stitches from holder to 2 double pointed needles. Rejoin yarns and knit these stitches in S&P. With another needle, pick up and knit 2 stitches in S&P at the base of the thumb (21 stitches). Arrange stitches on 3 needles. Note beginning of round. Work 15 rounds more in S&P, or until work reaches the tip of the thumb. Work Finger Decrease Rounds 1–2.

Finishing. Darn ends securely. Press lightly, omitting ribbing.

MOCKBEGGAR
Mittens for Youngsters

DEGREE OF DIFFICULTY: ✱ ✱ ✱ OVER THE WHARF

For centuries countless children have lived and played in and among the colourful houses of Mockbeggar (48.65°N, 53.18°W). Jutting precariously into the North Atlantic, it is indeed a windy, wild place to play. Folktales tell that at low tide at the tip of Mose's Point you can see the devil's cloven hoof in the solid bedrock. If that is not enough to send youngsters running home at dark, it gets even scarier. Around the corner is the main house of the Mockbeggar Plantation. It is said that a ghostly presence has been seen in the upstairs window on many occasions. And that is not all. At another house, a ghostly lady who died years before can be seen rocking in her chair. In another Mockbeggar home, doors open to let the occupants in at night, then shut behind them. These creepy tales may send chills all over, but our colourful cozy mittens will keep tiny hands warm. Mockbeggar Mittens use a main colour from start to finish and six contrast colours.

SIZE

2 to 4 years. Circumference: 6.50 inches (16.5 cm). Length measured from beginning of the Mockbeggar pattern to cast off: 4.75 inches (12 cm). Length is adjustable.

MATERIALS

Sport weight wool (Group 2). Oddments of main colour and 6 contrasting colours. 1 set each double pointed needles 2.75 mm and 3.00 mm. Place markers, stitch holders, and a medium-sized sharp darning needle. Samples shown were knit using Briggs and Little Sport 100% wool.

GAUGE

15 stitches = 2 inches (5 cm) worked in stocking stitch using 2.75 needles.

SALT AND PEPPER PATTERN (S&P)

Worked on an odd number of stitches.

Round 1. (K1M, K1C). Repeat to end of round.
Round 2. (K1C, K1M). Repeat to end of round.

How to Follow the Mockbeggar Chart. Work chart right to left, bottom to top until 3 tiers of houses are complete ending after row 24. Plan the colour scheme ahead. All houses may be the same colour or each tier a different colour, as in the samples shown.

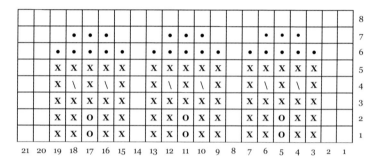

21	20	19	18	17	16	15	14	13	12	11	10	9	8	7	6	5	4	3	2	1	Row
																					8
			•	•	•				•	•	•				•	•	•				7
		•	•	•	•	•		•	•	•	•	•		•	•	•	•	•			6
		X	X	X	X	X		X	X	X	X	X		X	X	X	X	X			5
		X	\	X	\	X		X	\	X	\	X		X	\	X	\	X			4
		X	X	X	X	X		X	X	X	X	X		X	X	X	X	X			3
		X	X	O	X	X		X	X	O	X	X		X	X	O	X	X			2
		X	X	O	X	X		X	X	O	X	X		X	X	O	X	X			1

COLOUR LEGEND

Empty square = Main colour (M).

X House colour. Join at stitch 3 of row 1 and break after Round 5 is complete.

• Black roofs. Join on stitch 3 of row 6 and break after Round 8 is complete.

O Doors. Contrast colour of your choice. 12-inch (30 cm) lengths, 2 per tier of houses (6 total). Join on stitch 5 and drop after stitch 17. There is no need to carry this colour to end of round.

\ Windows. Yellow or Gold. 12-inch (30 cm) lengths. 1 per tier of houses (3 total). Join at stitch 4 and drop after stitch 18. There is no need to carry this colour to end of round.

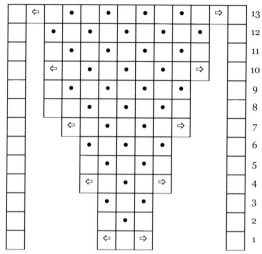

1	2	3	4	5	6	7	Row
⇐	•	•	•	•	•	⇒	13
	•	•	•	•	•		12
		•	•	•	•		11
⇐	•	•	•	•		⇒	10
		•	•	•	•		9
			•	•	•		8
	⇐	•	•		⇒		7
		•	•	•			6
			•	•			5
	⇐	•		⇒			4
		•	•				3
			•				2
	⇐		⇒				1

Empty square = M   • C

⇐ Make 1 Left with C   ⇒ Make 1 Right with C

Remember that the 21 stitches of the chart are referred to as rows, while the instructions for joining and breaking the colours of the houses, including roofs, is referred to as rounds.

Always keep main colour (M) to the left and all contrast colours (C) to the right to prevent colour streaks in the work.

Any time a colour must be carried behind more than three stitches, weave it in at the back as you proceed. This maintains the elasticity of the work.

Mockbeggar is a historically significant section of the town of Bonavista. It was the home of Senator F. Gordon Bradley, a father of Confederation who, along with former premier Joseph R. Smallwood, was responsible for signing Newfoundland into Canada on April 1, 1949. He lived in the main house of the Mockbeggar Plantation. This Provincial Historic Site, which contains a number of buildings in addition to the main house, was a fishing plantation from the 18th to the 20th century.

The Mockbeggar Plantation main house contains a library. This special room is home to a beautiful stained-glass window depicting the voyage Genoese explorer Giovanni Caboto (John Cabot) made here in 1497. It is widely believed that Cabot, who was working for the English, landed in Bonavista in his ship *The Matthew*. His alleged words, "O buono vista!" translated into English mean "O happy sight!"

Mockbeggar Plantation.

there is hop-scotch on the corner of the block

hopes of spring

young girls in bare heads with high pitched laughter

singing popular songs

old men repairing pots

young men launching boats

lobster season

—AGNES WALSH, IN *THE OLD COUNTRY OF MY HEART*

Wrist. With Main colour (M) and 2.75 mm double pointed needles, cast on 39 stitches. Join in a round, being careful not to twist.

Round 1. (K2, P1) repeat to end of round. Repeat this round in solid colour or stripes of your choice until the wrist measures 2 inches (5 cm). **Next Round.** (K2, P1) to end of round, increasing 5 stitches evenly spaced (44 stitches). Change to 3.00 mm double pointed needles.

RIGHT HAND ONLY

Arrange stitches on needles. Needle 1: 21 stitches (front of mitten). Needle 2: 12 stitches. Needle 3: 11 stitches. Join and break contrast colours as described above.

   Round 1. Needle 1. Work Row 1 of Mockbeggar chart (MC). Needle 2. Place marker, work Row 1 of Mockbeggar thumb gusset chart, place marker. Work Round 1 of S&P pattern to end of round. The Mockbeggar pattern is now positioned on the front of the mitten, the thumb gusset between the markers, and S&P on the palm. Continue working successive rows of MC on the front, thumb gusset as positioned, and S&P on palm until Round 13 is complete.

Round 14. Work Row 14 of MC, remove marker. Slip 13 stitches of the thumb gusset (including the 2 outline stitches) to a stitch holder. Cast on 4 stitches in the correct colour sequence to bridge the gap. Remove marker. Work S&P to the end of the round. (21 stitches on needle 1. Needles 2 and 3 share the 24 palm stitches.) Thumb gusset is now complete.

Continue to work MC on the front of the mitten and S&P on the palm until Round 24 is complete. Break all colours except M. Join contrast colour of your choice, work 2 rounds or desired number in S&P.

Slip 1 stitch from the beginning of needle 2 onto the end of needle 1 (22 front stitches). Needles 2 and 3 share the 23 palm stitches.

LEFT HAND ONLY

Round 1. Join yarns and work MC on needle 1 for front of the mitten. Needle 2. Work Round 1 of S&P pattern. Needle 3.

Continue Round 1 S&P pattern to last 3 stitches, place marker. Work Row 1 of Mockbeggar thumb gusset chart. Place marker.

Continue working successive rows of MC on the front of the mitten, S&P on the palm, and thumb gusset chart until round 13 is complete.

Round 14. Needle 1. Work Row 14 MC. Work S&P pattern to marker, remove marker. Slip 13 thumb gusset stitches (including the outline stitches) to a stitch holder. Cast on 4 stitches in correct colour sequence to bridge the gap. Thumb gusset is now complete.

Continue to work MC on the front of the mitten and S&P on the palm until Round 24 is complete. Slip the last stitch of Round 24 to the beginning of needle 1. Break all colours except M. Join contrast colour of your choice, work 2 rounds or desired number in S&P.

BOTH HANDS

Shape Top. On odd-numbered rounds, decreasing will create 2 adjacent stitches of the same colour. On the following even-numbered rounds, these stitches will be worked together, restoring the correct colour sequence. Decreases are made 1 stitch in from the edge at 4 points in the round.

Shaping Round 1. Needle 1. K1 in correct colour. SSK with the next colour in the sequence. Resume S&P pattern on the next stitch, having made 2 adjacent stitches of the same colour. Work in pattern until 3 stitches remain on the needle. K2tog in the same colour as the stitch just made. Work the last stitch in correct colour. **Needle 2.** K1, SSK as above, work in pattern to end of the needle. **Needle 3.** Work in pattern until 3 stitches remain before the end of the needle. K2tog in the same colour as the stitch just made. K1 in correct colour. **Shaping Round 2.** Work SSK and K2tog decreases in S&P at the same points as the previous round. Colour sequence will be restored.

Decrease in this manner until 13 stitches remain. Cast off, using 3-needle bind off.

3-Needle Bind Off. Place the stitches from the front of the mitten on a length of waste yarn. Place the stitches of the palm on another length of waste yarn. Turn the mitten inside out to work the bind off. Return the stitches from the threads to 2 thinner double pointed needles for convenience. Hold these needles parallel to one another. Have the needle with the greater number of stitches nearest you. With a third needle and using the long tail of M, K1 from the holding needle nearest you. Then knit 1 stitch from the front needle together with 1 stitch of the opposite colour from the back needle. You now have 2 stitches on the working needle. Pass the first stitch on the working needle over the second stitch to cast it off. 1 stitch remains on the working needle. Continue to knit together 1 stitch from the front and back needles and slipping the first stitch over the second stitch on the working needle to cast it off. Repeat until 1 stitch remains. Fasten off and darn in ends.

Thumb. Slip 13 gusset stitches from holder to 2 needles. Rejoin M and the contrast colour used for the roof. Knit these 13 stitches in correct colour sequence. With a third needle, pick up and knit in S&P pattern 6 stitches at the base of the mitten (19 stitches). Work 11 rounds more, or desired length, in S&P. **Thumb Decrease Round 1.** (Knit first stitch in correct colour sequence. K2tog with next colour, K1 with the same colour as the stitch just worked). Repeat to end of round, knitting any remaining stitches in S&P. **Thumb Decrease Round 2.** (K1, K2tog) in S&P to the end of the round, working any remaining stitches in S&P. Break yarns, draw up, and fasten securely.

Finishing. Turn mittens inside out. Carefully darn in the many ends securely, checking that none is too loose or too tight. Turn right side out and check again. Lightly press, omitting ribbing.

© Christine LeGrow 2019

BRIGUS
Boot Socks for Ladies

DEGREE OF DIFFICULTY: ✳✳ TANGLY

Brigus (47.53°N, 53.22°W) is a small fishing community on Conception Bay, Newfoundland. Settled in 1612, it retains its quaint appeal to the present day. It is the birthplace of famous Arctic explorer Captain Bob Bartlett. Hawthorne Cottage, his family home, is a National Historic Site open to visitors. A tunnel bored through solid rock in 1860 provided easy access to a deepwater berth for his sailing ships and continues to be a landmark attraction. After a life of research, exploration, and receiving numerous accolades, Bartlett passed away in 1946 and is buried in his hometown.

Besides seafaring explorers Brigus is known for its plump, juicy, wild blueberries that grow in abundance and provide an occasion for the annual Brigus Blueberry Festival. A stone barn, many beautiful churches from past centuries, and a working forge enrich an interesting walk around this picturesque town.

The hiking trail to the Brigus lighthouse inspired the Brigus Boot Socks. The honeycomb design at the top of the sock brings summer wildflowers buzzing with bees to memory. The top of this snug fitting boot sock has a flexible open back to fit over a short hiking boot. The cables bordering the opening call to mind ropes anchoring ships to shore.

SIZE

Ladies' Medium. Length of foot from heel to tip of toe: 9.5 inches (24 cm). Foot length is adjustable.

MATERIALS

400 metres of medium worsted weight wool (Group 4). 1 pair very strong 4.00 mm needles 12.5 inches (32 cm) long. 1 set 3.50 mm double pointed needles. 1 set 4.00 mm double pointed needles. 1 cable needle. 1 place marker and 1 sharp darning needle.

GAUGE

9 stitches = 2 inches (5 cm) in stocking stitch using 4.00 mm needles.

BRIGUS HONEYCOMB CABLE PATTERN (BHC)

80 stitches.

Worked flat.

Row 1. P1, K6, P1. *C4B (= slip 2 stitches to cable needle and leave at back of work. K2, K2 stitches from the cable needle). C4F (= slip 2 stitches to cable needle and leave at front of work. K2, K2 stitches from the cable needle)*. Repeat from * to * 7 times more. P1, K6, P1 (80 stitches).

Row 2. K1, P6, K1. Purl to last 8 stitches. K1, P6, K1.

Row 3. P1, K6, P1. Knit to last 8 stitches. P1, K6, P1.

Row 4. As Row 2.

Row 5. P1, C6B (= slip 3 stitches to a cable needle and leave at back of work. K3, K3 stitches from the cable needle), P1. (C4F, C4B) 7 times more. P1, C6F (= slip 3 stitches to a cable needle and leave at front of work. K3, K3 stitches from cable needle), P1.

Row 6. As Row 2.

Row 7. As Row 3.

Row 8. As Row 2.

Begin the boot sock with two needles and knit back and forth until honeycomb pattern on boot top is complete. The remainder of the sock is in the round.

Boot Top. With strong 4.00 mm long needles, cast on 80 stitches. Working back and forth, work 16 rows in BHC pattern.
Work rows 1 to 5 of BHC pattern.

Next Row. Work 40 stitches of Row 6 of BHC pattern. Place marker. Work last 40 stitches of BHC pattern.

Decrease Round. P1, K1, K2tog, K2tog, K1, P1, [K1, K2tog, K2tog]. Repeat (to) until 2 stitches remain before marker. K2tog, slip marker. SSK, [SSK, SSK, K1]. Repeat (to) until 8 stitches remain. P1, K1, SSK, SSK, K1, P1 (50 stitches). This completes the boot top.

Join in a Round. With **wrong** side of the BHC pattern facing, knit to the marker, decreasing 4 stitches evenly spaced. Remove marker. Knit to end of row, decreasing 4

more stitches evenly spaced. Without turning work, change to 3.50 mm double pointed needles as follows. Slip 11 stitches to needle 1, 20 stitches to needle 2, 11 stitches to needle 3. Join in a round (42 stitches).

Next Round. (K1, P1). Repeat to end of round. Repeat this round 21 times more. Changing to 4.00 mm double pointed needles, knit 7 rounds.

Arrange Heel Stitches. Slip 10 of the instep stitches on needle 2 to a spare needle and leave them to be worked later. Knit the 11 stitches from needle 1 on to the end of needle 3.

Heel Flap. Worked flat. Working on these 22 stitches, with wrong side facing, K1, P9, P2tog, P9, K1 (21 stitches).

Row 1. Right side. (K1, slip 1) being careful not to tighten the yarn behind the slipped stitch. Repeat to last stitch, K1.
Row 2. Wrong side. K1, purl to last stitch, K1.
Repeat these 2 rows 8 times more. Work Row 1 once.

Turn Heel. Row 1. P12, P2tog, P1. Turn. **Row 2.** K5, SKP, K1. Turn. **Row 3.** P6, P2tog, P1. Turn. **Row 4.** K7, SKP, K1. Turn. **Row 5.** P8, P2tog, P1. Turn. **Row 6.** K9, SKP, K1. Turn. **Row 7.** P10, P2tog, P1. Turn. **Row 8.** K11, SKP, K1 (13 stitches).

Instep. Pick Up Stitches. Transfer the 20 instep stitches back to one needle. Needle 1. With right side of work facing, and using the needle containing the 13 heel stitches, pick up and knit 10 stitches along the edge of the heel flap. Needle 2. Knit. Needle 3. Pick up and knit 10 stitches along the remaining edge of the heel flap. Knit 6 stitches from needle 1. (Needle 1: 17, needle 2: 20, needle 3: 16).

Decrease Instep. Round 1. Knit. **Round 2.** Needle 1. Knit until 3 stitches remain on needle, K2tog, K1. Needle 2. Knit. Needle 3. K1, SKP, knit to end of needle. Repeat Rounds 1 and 2 until 39 stitches remain. (Needle 1: 10, needle 2: 20, needle 3: 9).

Continue in stocking stitch, without decreasing, until work measures 6 inches (14 cm), or desired length from pick-

Picking Up Stitches. Inserting the needle through the knot formed by the knitted stitch at the beginning and end of each row of the heel flap, then knitting into the back of it, will prevent a hole forming.

up round. Knit 1 round, decreasing 1 stitch at the centre.

Shape Toe. Round 1. Needle 1. Knit until 3 stitches remain, K2tog, K1. Needle 2. K1, SKP, knit until 3 stitches remain, K2tog, K1. Needle 3. K1, SKP, knit to end of needle. **Round 2.** Knit.

Repeat these 2 rounds until 14 stitches remain. Knit the remaining stitches from needle 1 on to the end of needle 3. Break yarn, leaving a tail 12 inches long.

Graft Toe. Thread the long tail of yarn through the darning needle. Hold work so that the long tail of yarn is to the right and on the rear holding needle. Insert the darning needle into

Nan AT YOUR Side

After you determine which comfy boots to wear them with, sew the back seam if desired (not shown). To sew the seam, have the wrong side of the boot top facing you. Sew the selvedges together, neatly darning the ends when complete.

the first stitch on the front holding needle as if to knit, draw it though this stitch and slip it off the knitting needle. Insert the darning needle as if to purl into the next stitch on the front needle and pull the yarn though but leave the stitch on the knitting needle.

Take the yarn under the front holding needle and insert the darning needle into the first stitch on the rear holding needle as if to purl. Draw it from the holding needle. Insert the darning needle into the next stitch on the rear holding needle as if to knit, draw the yarn through but leave that stitch on the holding needle.

Returning to the front knitting needle, continue in this manner until all the stitches have been removed from both holding needles. Darn in the end securely.

Finishing. Darn ends. Turn the boot top down at the fold mark. Omitting the boot top and ankle ribbing, gently press the foot of the sock.

© Christine LeGrow 2019

Diamond Vamps from Little Heart's Ease.

THE GREAT VAMP DEBATE

Boots, snowshoes, buskins, and vamps were the winter footwear of early Newfoundland, a system of layering that kept feet warm and dry in the worst of conditions. Keeping legs and feet dry was a huge concern. Newfoundland remained untouched by modern winter footwear for a long time, ingenuity replacing manufactured goods. Boots were often homemade, traditionally from skin or hide with sheep's wool for lining. Sometimes a knitted buskin or "gaiter" was worn over a boot, possibly for traction. Buskins and gaiters have disappeared from today's winter wear but the others remain.

"You'd make the boots a couple of sizes too large for your foot and then you'd get on some vamps. Sometimes they'd have skin vamps and then a woolen one inside, besides the sock."

—*DICTIONARY OF NEWFOUNDLAND ENGLISH*

BUSKIN

Covering for the foot and leg; leather gaiters; a cloth or woolen gaiter or legging worn to keep snow out of boots.

"Several women on the Southern Shore claimed that they knitted a type of oversock that was worn over the boot and extended up almost to the knee on the outside of the pants. These were also worn by men when they went into the forest to gather firewood. They were commonly called buskins."

—*DICTIONARY OF NEWFOUNDLAND ENGLISH*

Vamps.

Knitted layers, in the form of socks and vamps, were worn inside the boot. The *Dictionary of Newfoundland English* suggests that a vamp is a short, thick oversock worn in boots to prevent chafing (also known as "rinding out"), or around the house as a slipper. Shoes and boots were large to accommodate these insulating layers and were then often handed down, so perfect-fitting footwear was rare. Aside from adding warmth, a pair of vamps worn in boots eased the fit when they were too big.

When is a vamp not a vamp? When it's a sock or a slipper, of course. Distinguishing socks from vamps is far from simple. Sometimes it's just a question of the length. How short is short? But like many things in Newfoundland culture, it may also depend on where you live. A vamp that covers the foot just to the instep with a very short snug-fitting ribbed cuff to

keep it from slipping off is at home in Bonavista Proper. A little farther along the road in Mockbeggar any thick hand-knit sock of any leg length is called a vamp.

Are vamps outerwear or house wear? Passions run high on this question. While they are certainly often worn as slippers, vamps do not necessarily cancel out socks. Some people wear the two, in the house or outdoors in a pair of boots. This spreads the wear around, a very good idea as darning was a major occupation in days gone by. Some swear that vamps stayed always in the boots, ready for a quick exit. We conclude that vamps save wear on your feet, and possibly on your socks too.

In *Saltwater Classics* we embrace all definitions and have provided patterns for several versions. But the great vamp debate continues. It's tangly.

Family Vamps.

FAMILY VAMPS
in Four Sizes

DEGREE OF DIFFICULTY: ✳ EASY DOES IT

The amount of hand-knit footwear needed for a large family is hard to comprehend, especially vamps, which were worn all year long. There were no idle hands in those days. Fancy double vamps were sometimes knit, but a reliable basic pattern that could be quickly made up in many sizes was essential.

The style of your vamp sometimes proclaimed your place of origin. Bonavista Proper is the centre part of the town of Bonavista, Newfoundland (48.65°N, 53.11°W). If you were born in or lived in this part of the town, you would proudly say you were from Bonavista Proper and would probably wear these family vamps. They cover only the foot to the instep with a short, snug-fitting cuff to keep them from slipping off. Were the cuff any longer it would be considered an ankle sock. In another part of town known as Mockbeggar, all hand-knit thick wool socks regardless of leg length were referred to as vamps. Imagine the confusion when a young maiden from Mockbeggar married a young lad from Bonavista Proper and he requested some vamps!

SIZE

Instructions include four sizes. The pattern is written for the smallest size (XS), with the three additional sizes marked as indicated, (S) youngsters', (M) medium, (L) large.

Foot from heel to tip of toe. XS: 7 inches (18 cm), S: 8.5 inches (21.5 cm), M: 9.5 inches (24 cm), L: 10.5 inches (27 cm). Foot length is adjustable.

MATERIALS

Medium worsted weight wool (Group 4). Sizes XS and S: 100 metres. Size M: 125 metres. Size L: 200 metres. 1 set each of 3.50 mm and 4.00 mm double pointed needles. Sharp darning needle. Samples were knit with Briggs and Little Heritage 100% wool.

GAUGE

9 stitches = 2 inches (5 cm) worked in stocking stitch, using 4.00 mm needles.

Cuff. Where only one number is given, it applies to all sizes. With 3.50 mm double pointed needles, cast on as follows and join in round, being careful not to twist.

XS. 34 stitches. Arrange stitches 12, 10, 12.

S. 38 stitches. Arrange stitches 12, 14, 12.

M. 42 stitches. Arrange stitches 14, 14, 14.

L. 46 stitches. Arrange stitches 14, 18, 14.

Round 1. (K1, P1) to end of round. Work 7 (7, 9, 9) more rounds in rib. Change to 4.00 mm needles.

Arrange heel stitches. Slip 3 (2, 3, 2) stitches from the end of needle 1 to beginning of needle 2. Slip 3 (2, 3, 2) stitches from the beginning of needle 3 to the end of needle 2. Stitches are thus arranged as follows.

XS. 9, 16, 9.

S. 10, 18, 10.

M. 11, 20, 11.

L. 12, 22, 12.

Divide stitches on the second needle on 2 needles and set aside for instep, to be worked later.

Rib remaining stitches from needle 1 to the end of needle 3, increasing 1 stitch in the last stitch. Working on these 19 (21, 23, 25) stitches, begin heel flap.

Heel Flap. Set Up. Worked flat. K1, P17 (19, 21, 23), K1. **Row 1.** Right side. (K1, Slip 1) to last stitch, K1. Do not tighten the yarn behind the slipped stitch as you work. **Row 2.** Wrong side. K1, purl to last stitch, K1. Repeat these 2 rows 6 (8, 9, 10) times more. **Next Row.** As Row 1.

Turn Heel. Row 1. Wrong side. K1, P9 (10, 11, 11), P2tog, P1. Turn. **Row 2.** Right side. K3, SKP, K1. Turn. **Row 3.** P4, P2tog, P1. Turn. **Row 4.** K5, SKP, K1. Turn. **Row 5.** P6, P2tog, P1. Turn. **Row 6.** K7, SKP, K1. Turn. **Row 7.** P8, P2tog, P1. Turn. **Row 8.** K9, SKP, K1.

Complete Heel.

XS only. 11 stitches remain on the needle. Proceed to Instep.

S only. Row 9. P10, P2tog. Turn. **Row 10.** K10, SKP. 11 stitches remain on the needle. Proceed to Instep.

M only. Row 9. P10, P2tog, P1. Turn. **Row 10.** K11, SKP, K1. 13 stitches remain on the needle. Proceed to Instep.

L only. Row 9. P10, P2 tog. P1. Turn. **Row 10.** K11, SKP, K1. Turn. **Row 11.** P12, P2tog. P1. Turn. **Row 12.** K12, SKP. 13 stitches remain on the needle. Proceed to Instep.

Nan AT YOUR Side

To prevent holes when picking up stitches along the side of this heel, insert the working needle through the knot of the knitted stitch at the beginning and end of each row of the heel flap.

Instep. Set Up. Transfer 16 (18, 20, 22) stitches reserved for the instep to one needle. Needle 1. With right side facing pick up and knit 9 (10, 11, 12) stitches along the side of the heel. Needle 2. Knit 16 (18, 20, 22) stitches. Needle 3. Pick up and knit 9 (10, 11, 12) stitches along the second side of the heel. Knit 5 (5, 6, 6) stitches from the beginning of Needle 1.

Stitches are now arranged as follows. Needle 1. 15 (16, 18, 19) stitches. Needle 2. 16 (18, 20, 22) stitches. Needle 3. 14 (15, 17, 18) stitches.

Complete Instep. Round 1. Knit. **Round 2.** Needle 1. Knit to last 3 stitches, K2tog. K1. Needle 2. Knit. Needle 3. K1, SKP, knit to end of needle.

Repeat these two rounds until 31 (35, 39, 43) stitches remain in round, distributed as follows. Needle 1. 8 (9, 10, 11) stitches. Needle 2. 16 (18, 20, 22) stitches. Needle 3. 7 (8, 9, 10) stitches.

Continue in stocking stitch until work measures 5 (5.5, 6, 6.5) inches, or desired length from instep pick up round. **Next Round.** Needle 1. Knit. Needle 2. Knit to centre 2 stitches, K2tog, knit to end of needle. Needle 3. Knit.

Toe. Round 1. Needle 1. Knit to last 3 stitches, K2tog, K1.

Needle 2. K1, SKP, knit to last 3 stitches, K2tog, K1. Needle 3. K1, SKP, knit to end of needle. **Round 2.** Knit to end of round.

Repeat these 2 rounds until 10 (10, 14, 14) stitches remain in the round, ending with Round 2. Knit the stitches from needle 1 onto the end of needle 3. Break yarn leaving a tail approximately 12 inches long for grafting and darning the toe.

Graft Toe. Hold work so that the long tail of yarn is to your right and on the back holding needle. Insert the darning needle into the first stitch on the front holding needle as if to knit. Draw it though this stitch and slip it off the needle. Insert the darning needle into the next stitch on the front needle as if to purl and pull yarn though but leave the stitch on the holding needle. Take the yarn under the front needle and insert the darning needle into the first stitch on the back holding needle as if to purl. Draw it off the needle. Insert the darning needle into the next stitch on the back holding needle as if to knit. Draw the yarn through but leave that stitch on the holding needle. Return to the front holding needle and continue in this manner until all stitches have been removed from both holding needles. Darn the end securely.

Finishing. Darn ends. Press lightly, omitting ribbing.

© Christine LeGrow 2019

TREASURE TROUT
Baby Vamps

DEGREE OF DIFFICULTY: ✳✳ TANGLY

Treasure Trout is a loving term for babies in Newfoundland. "How is Nanny's little treasure trout today?" grandmothers might ask. Tiny treasure trouts need vamps to keep little toes warm. Knit from oddments of sport weight wool, many geometric patterns are possible. Here are three delightful ones to choose from—blocks, dots, and a fancy one too. Two contrasting colours are all you need.

SIZE

Infant 3 to 6 months. Foot from beginning of heel to tip of toe: 4.5 inches (11 cm).

MATERIALS

50 metres of sport weight wool (Group 2) in Dark (D). Approximately 50 metres sport weight wool (Group 2) in Light (L). Samples were knit with Briggs and Little Sport. One set 2.75 mm double pointed needles. Sharp darning needle.

GAUGE

15 stitches = 2 inches (5 cm) worked in stocking stitch using 2.75 mm needles.

SALT AND PEPPER PATTERN (S&P)

Worked on an odd number of stitches.

Round 1. (K1D, K1L). Repeat to last stitch, K1D.

Round 2. (K1L, K1D). Repeat to last stitch, K1L.

How to Follow the Blocks Chart. Work Rounds 1 to 8 twice, then Rounds 1 to 4 once (20 rounds).

How to Follow the Dots Chart. Work Rounds 1 to 8 twice, then Rounds 1 to 4 once (20 rounds).

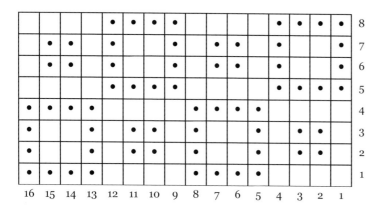

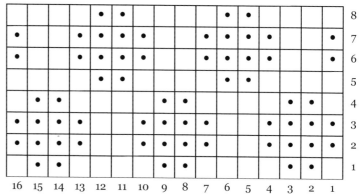

Blocks.

Dots.

Fancy.

TREASURE TROUT FANCY CHART

How to Follow the Fancy Chart. Work Rounds 1 to 6 three times, then Round 1 once (19 rounds).

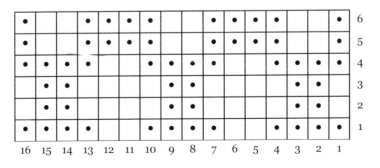

16	15	14	13	12	11	10	9	8	7	6	5	4	3	2	1	
•			•	•	•	•			•	•	•	•			•	6
•			•	•	•	•				•	•	•	•		•	5
•	•	•	•				•	•	•	•			•	•	•	4
	•	•				•	•						•	•		3
	•	•				•	•						•	•		2
•	•	•	•			•	•	•	•			•	•	•	•	1

• K1D   Empty square = K1L

Read charts right to left and bottom to top. Always carry D to the left and L to the right to prevent streaks in your colour work.

With D cast on 36 stitches. Join in a round being careful not to twist. **Round 1.** (K2, P1). Repeat to end of round. Repeat this round in solid colour or in stripes until the cuff measures 2 inches (5 cm) from cast on edge.

Arrange Heel Stitches. Slip 2 stitches purlwise from the end of needle 1 to the beginning of needle 2. Slip 2 stitches purlwise from the beginning of needle 3 to the end of needle 2. Divide these stitches on 2 needles and reserve for instep. Knit the remaining stitches from needle 1 onto the end of needle 3. **Next Row.** Working on these 20 stitches, K1, P8, P2tog, P8, K1 (19 stitches for heel flap).

Heel Flap. Worked flat. **Row 1.** Right side. (K1, slip 1). Being careful not to tighten the yarn carried behind the slipped stitches, repeat until 1 stitch remains. K1. **Row 2.** Wrong side. K1, purl to last stitch, K1. Repeat these 2 rows 6 times more. **Next Row.** Repeat Heel Flap Row 1 once.

Turn Heel. Row 1. Wrong side. K1, P9, P2tog, P1. Turn. **Row 2.** Right side. K3, SKP, K1. Turn. **Row 3.** P4, P2tog, P1. Turn. **Row 4.** K5, SKP, K1. Turn. **Row 5.** P6, P2tog, P1. Turn. **Row 6.** K7, SKP, K1. Turn. **Row 7.** P8, P2tog, P1. Turn. **Row 8.** K9, SKP, K1 (11 stitches remain).

Instep. Set-Up Round. Transfer 16 instep stitches to one needle.

Needle 1. With right side of work facing, and using the needle containing the 11 heel stitches, join L. Pick up and knit 9 stitches while working Round 1 of S&P pattern along the side of the heel flap, being careful to avoid creating holes. Needle 2. Knit Round 1 of Treasure Trout chart of your choice. Needle 3. Beginning with K1L, pick up and knit 9 stitches in S&P along the other side of the heel flap. Knit 6 stitches from the bottom of the heel on to the end of needle 3. (Needle 1: 14 S&P stitches. Needle 2: 16 Treasure Trout stitches. Needle 3. 15 S&P stitches.)

Instep Round 1. Needle 1. Work the remaining 5 D stitches at the beginning of needle 1 in the correct S&P colour sequence to the end of needle 1. Needle 2. Work Round 2 of Treasure Trout. Needle 3. Work in S&P.

Instep Round 2. Needle 1. Work S&P pattern to last 3 stitches. K2 tog using the same colour as the stitch just worked. K1 in correct colour sequence. Needle 2. Work Round 3 of Treasure Trout. Needle 3. K1 in correct colour sequence. SSK in next colour in the sequence. K1 in colour just worked. Continue in S&P to end of the needle.

Instep Round 3. Needle 1. Work S&P pattern to last 3 stitches. K2tog in next colour in sequence. K1 in correct colour in sequence. Needle 2. Work Row 4 of Treasure Trout. Needle 3. K1 in correct colour in sequence; SSK in next colour in sequence. Continue in S&P to end of needle.

Nan
AT YOUR
Side

If you have many oddments of yarn to use up, choose the Dots pattern. Dots may be a different colour for each vertical repeat of the pattern. At the end of Round 4 break D. At the beginning of Round 5 join a new colour to substitute for D. At the end of Round 8 break this contrast colour. Join another oddment at the beginning of the following Round 1. Continue adding new colours until 20 rounds of Dots are complete.

Continue decreasing on needles 1 and 3, having no decreases on one round followed by 2 rounds with decreases at both sides of the instep. Work successive rounds of Treasure Trout on needle 2.

Work until needle 1 has 8 stitches, needle 2 has 16 stitches, and needle 3 has 9 stitches (33 stitches).

Continue in S&P on the sole of the foot and Treasure Trout on the front until 20 rounds (19 for Fancy) of Treasure Trout pattern has been worked ending with needle 3. Break L.

Toe. Next Round. Needle 1: Knit. Needle 2: Knit. Needle 3: Knit to last 2 stitches, K2tog.

Round 1. Needle 1. Knit until 3 stitches remain, K2tog, K1. Needle 2. K1, SKP, knit to last 3 stitches, K2tog, K1. Needle 3. K1, SKP, K to end of needle. **Round 2.** Knit.

Repeat Rounds 1 and 2 until 16 stitches remain in the round, ending with Round 2. Knit the 4 stitches from needle 1 on to the end of needle 3. Break yarn, leaving a 12-inch tail.

Graft Toe. Thread the long tail of yarn through the darning needle. Hold work so that the long tail of yarn is to the right and on the back needle. Insert the darning needle into the first stitch on the front holding needle as if to knit. Draw yarn though this stitch and slip it off the holding needle. Insert the darning needle into the next stitch on the front holding needle as if to purl. Draw yarn though but leave this stitch on the holding needle.

Move yarn under the front needle and insert the darning needle into the first stitch on the back holding needle as if to purl. Draw stitch off the back needle. Insert the darning needle into the next stitch on the back needle as if to knit. Draw the yarn through but leave that stitch on the back holding needle.

Return to the front knitting needle and continue in this manner until all stitches have been removed from both knitting needles.

Finishing. Darn ends. Press lightly, omitting ribbing.

© Christine LeGrow 2019

His and Hers DIAMOND VAMPS
From LITTLE HEART'S EASE

DEGREE OF DIFFICULTY: ✳ ✳ ✳ OVER THE WHARF

Little Heart's Ease (48.0°N, 53.7°W) is one charming community associated with the production of these sturdy vamps. Apart from the ribbed leg portion every part of the garment is knit with two colours in double ball knitting. For this reason, they are often called "double vamps." They are twice as warm and last much longer than single slipper socks. The larger size is made simply by using heavier yarn and bigger needles.

Love a challenge? For this design, we first decoded then replicated a pair of vintage vamps down to the last detail. Even experienced sock knitters will find a few brain teasers here. The toe, for example, has a picket-fence shaping, as on a classic Newfoundland mitten. Short and sweet, it is decreased on every round to a gentle point. This style likely evolved as an alternative to grafting the toe in two colours. It fits surprisingly well and the point moderates with wear. The instep is also speedily decreased on every round. With a heel flap worked flat in fairisle, instep stitches picked up and decreased in skill-testing salt and pepper pattern, and a few more clever tricks thrown in for good measure, we are quite certain that the knitters who first developed this design knew their stuff. Allow yourself the luxury of a long learning curve and make several pairs.

Remember, vamps make very slippery slippers. So slippery that youngsters were often asked to wear them to polish newly waxed floors. Take care when wearing them.

"I was sittin' by myself in the kitchen this night about nine o'clock. With my boots off, a pair of woolen vamps hauled on over my socks, with my feet up on the pan of the stove smokin' my pipe."

—*DICTIONARY OF NEWFOUNDLAND ENGLISH*

SIZE

HIS Men's Medium. Circumference of leg: 10 inches (26 cm) unstretched. Length of vamp from beginning of Diamond pattern to tip of toe: 9 inches (23 cm), or desired length. Length of leg: 6.5 inches (16.5 cm) or desired length. Depth of toe shaping: 3 inches (7.5 cm), or desired length. **HIS** is made by knitting **HERS** using larger needles and heavier yarn.

HERS Ladies' Medium. Circumference of leg: 9 inches (13 cm) without stretch. Length of vamp from beginning of Diamonds pattern to tip of toe: 8.5 inches (22 cm) or desired length. Length of leg: 3 inches (7.5 cm) or desired length. Depth of toe shaping: 2.5 inches (6 cm).

MATERIALS

HIS 2 or more shades of medium worsted weight wool (Group 4), 250 metres Dark (D), 250 metres Light (L). Oddments of L may be sufficient. For custom sizes more may be needed.

Samples were knit in Briggs and Little Heritage. 1 set of 5.00 mm double pointed needles.

HERS 2 or more shades of light worsted weight wool (Group 3), 125 metres Dark (D), 125 metres Light (L). Oddments of L may be sufficient. For custom sizes more may be needed. Samples were knit in Briggs and Little Regal. 1 set of 4.00 mm double pointed needles.

GAUGE

HERS 24 stitches and 28 rows = 4 inches (10 cm).
HIS 22 stitches and 24 rows = 4 inches (10 cm).

Diamond Vamps, Blue Moon.

DIAMOND CHART

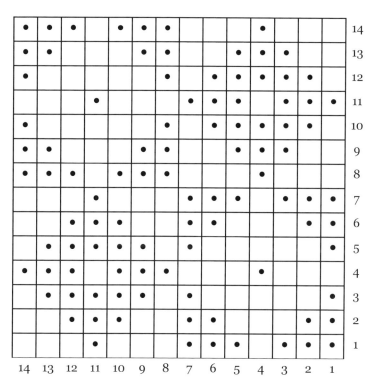

• K1D   Empty square = K1L

If desired, begin a new shade of L on Row 8 and on the following Row 1.

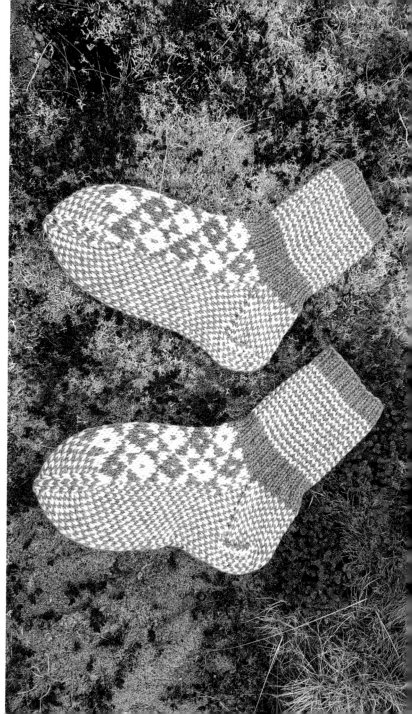

SALT AND PEPPER PATTERN (S&P)

Worked on an odd number of stitches.

Round 1. (K1 with D, K1 with L). Repeat to end of round.

Round 2. (K1L, K1D). Repeat to end of round.

Instructions are for **HERS** followed by **HIS.** If only one number appears it applies to both sizes. Read all charts from right to left, bottom to top. Always carry D ahead (i.e., on the left) to prevent streaks in work.

Leg. Cast on 54 stitches. Divide on 3 needles being careful not to twist. Work in (K2, P1) rib in a striped pattern of your choice for 3 inches, or desired length. Because they are usually worn over another sock vamps are roomy at the top and ankle. For a tighter fitting leg, choose a different ribbing.

Place the first 28 stitches on 2 double pointed needles for the front of the vamp. Leave the remaining 26 stitches on a single double pointed needle for the heel flap. Round begins at the ankle.

If your heel flap and heel stitches are uneven when working flat fairisle, drop each yarn after making a stitch with it, just for the few rows of the heel flap and heel. This way of knitting fairisle is slower than molasses in January but can be neater. Make sure to continue to carry D on the left throughout.

Heel Flap. Worked flat. **Next Round.** Turn work. With the wrong side facing, purl the stitches of the heel flap with D, increasing 1 stitch purlwise in the middle of the row (27 stitches). Turn.

Diamond Vamps, Nautical Blood.

Heel Flap Row 1. Right side. Join L. Working back and forth on heel flap stitches only work (K1D, K1L) to last stitch, K1D (27 stitches). Turn. **Heel Flap Row 2.** Wrong side. (P1L, P1D) to last stitch, P1L. Turn.

Working back and forth in S&P repeat Rows 1 and 2 until 16 rows of S&P are complete, ending with a wrong side row. **Turn Heel. Next Row.** Right side. Knit 19 stitches in S&P. Slip the next stitch knitwise. Slip the following stitch purlwise. With next colour in the S&P sequence, knit these 2 stitches together through the back loop. Turn.

Turning Row 1. Wrong side. Purl 12 stitches in S&P. With the next colour in the sequence purl the next 2 stitches together. Turn. **Turning Row 2.** Right side. Knit 12 in S&P. Slip the next stitch knitwise. Slip the following stitch purlwise. With next colour in the S&P sequence, knit these 2 stitches together through the back loop. Turn.

Repeat Turning Rows 1 and 2 until all heel flap stitches are incorporated into the heel, ending with Turning Row 1 (13 stitches). **Next Row.** With right side facing, knit 13 heel stitches in S&P.

Instep. Pick-Up Round. Right side. Beginning with K1D over an L stitch, pick up and knit 16 stitches along the side of the heel flap in S&P.

Place stitches of the front on a single needle. Work

Nan
AT YOUR
Side

Picking up instep stitches in pattern is some fun, isn't it? Even for an accomplished knitter. Will I find the correct colour where I need it? Will I find the correct number of stitches in the right order?

Nan says to select a vertical line of loops to pick up and stick to it. No jumping around. Pick up these stitches with a spare needle in advance, without knitting them. When the time comes to knit them, the correct number and colour of stitches will be ready for the magic touch. We all find our favourite places to pick up stitches, but Nan is firm about one thing. Never pick up stitches at the extreme edges of the heel flap unless you are a very good vamp knitter. Find nice, firm stitches inside the selvedge edge. It's safer. Think of each stitch as a heart and stab the needle boldly into the middle of it. Be consistent. Even though human nature goes against it.

Rock 'n' Roll colours.

Diamond chart 2 times on these stitches.

Beginning with K1D over an L stitch, pick up and knit 16 stitches in S&P along the remaining edge of the heel flap (73 stitches). Work S&P on heel and instep stitches, dividing stitches on two needles for convenience. The round now begins at the first Diamond stitch. Note new beginning of round.

Instep Decrease Round 1. Work Round 2 of Diamond chart twice on the front.

K1 in S&P. SSK with next colour in the sequence. K1 in correct colour of S&P. There will be 2 adjacent stitches of the same colour. This will be corrected on the following round. Work in S&P until 3 stitches remain in round. K2tog with same colour as the stitch just made. There will be 2 adjacent stitches of the same colour. K1 in S&P.

Instep Decrease Round 2. Work next round of Diamond twice on front. K1 in S&P. SSK with the next colour in the sequence. Work in S&P until 3 stitches remain in round. K2tog with the next colour in the sequence. K1 in S&P. Colour sequence is restored.

Working successive rounds of Diamond on the front, repeat Instep Decrease Rounds 1 and 2 until 57 stitches remain, ending with Round 2 (28 front, 29 sole).

Continue in patterns as set, without decreasing, until 35 rounds of Diamond pattern are complete on front, finishing the round in S&P.

Toe. Beginning with K1L, work S&P on front. Work S&P on sole. Work additional rounds of S&P if desired until work reaches 2.5 inches (**HIS** 3 inches) from desired tip of toe.

Shape Picket-Fence Toe. Shaping Round 1. K1 with correct S&P colour. SSK with next colour in the sequence, having made 2 adjacent stitches of the same colour. Work S&P until 3 stitches remain on needle. K2tog with the same colour as the stitch just made. K1 in correct colour of S&P. **Sole.** K1 with correct S&P colour. SSK with next colour in the sequence. Work S&P until 3 stitches remain in round. K2tog with the same colour as the stitch just made. K1 in correct colour of S&P. **Shaping Round 2.** K1, SSK in next colour in the sequence. S&P until 3 stitches remain on front. K2tog in next colour in the sequence, K1. **Sole.** As front. Correct colour sequence is restored.

Repeat these 2 shaping rounds until 9 stitches remain. Break yarns, leaving a long tail of one colour. Thread through loops, pull tight, and secure.

Finishing. Press firmly under a damp cloth. Do not press ribbing.

© Shirley A. Scott 2019

Drying.

ACKNOWLEDGEMENTS AND THANKS

Some of Newfoundland's many remarkable photographers contributed much to the beauty of this book. Anja Sajovic of Anja Sajovic Photography took the amazing cover and author photos. Others who kindly contributed photographs include Terry Adey, Paul Dunne, Shawn Fitzpatrick, Jack Foley, Walter George, Mary Dawn Greenwood, Jeanette Laaning, Derrick C. LeGrow, Derrick L. LeGrow, Laurie LeGrow, Marian Norris and Dave Burley, Urve Manual, and Jennifer Power.

Excellent models brought to life many designs in this book. A round of applause for cover models Stacey Benoit and Lora Cullen. Praise is in order for the great work of Derrick C. LeGrow, Derrick L. LeGrow, Serena LeGrow, Geri Ottenheimer, Janalynn Petten, Jessika Petten, and Laura Walker. Thanks to the wonderful Wind at Your Back Hiking Group, whose members include Lori Belbin, Tara Bishop, Marilyn Branton-Short, Taylor Hutchings, Barbara Parsons, Samantha Reid, Ryan Snelgrove, Linda Sooley, Susan Sooley-Snelgrove, and Debbie Tuttle. Heartiest thanks to show-stealers Boots and Brutus, the intrepid cats.

Help of all kinds comes in so many generous ways. Thanks to the Alexis Templeton Studio for the loan of the magnificent bicycle, to Lee Ann Fleming for her exquisite table linens, Anne Lucas of Foggy Rock Fibres for the luscious hand-dyed yarn featured in Family Vamps, and Lynn and Robert Young at Celebrity Photo for ably digitalizing the Trinity window photo. Zen Kader and Nora and Ruby Hiscock provided help with young sizes. Milly Brown, AnnMarie MacCrae, and Mary Dawn Greenwood contributed some uniquely beautiful shadings to this adventure in colour. Thanks to Dale Jarvis for his sensitive Foreword and Paul Doucet for his words of wisdom. We are grateful to Janice May for sharing her heartwarming story "Barrel Night in Montreal." Last but not least, we thank the Johnson Geo Centre for their backdrop of fabulous rocks. We are *connoisseurs* of rock in Newfoundland and this is a spectacular location for photography.

Our valiant test knitters had a big job on their never-idle hands. Suzanne Molloy, Denise Moss, Laurie LeGrow, and Milly Brown deserve much praise for their sharp eyes and excellent knitting skills.

"The Polar Star," by Isabella Whiteford, was published in

Whiteford's Poems (Belfast: M'Cormick & Dunlop, 1859).

"Old Crooked Fellow" appears in *Escape Velocity*, by Carmelita McGrath (Goose Lane Editions, 2013).

Special thanks to David Blackwood for permission to publish *Home from Bragg's Island* and to The Rooms for making the image available. *Home from Bragg's Island,* 2009; oil tempera on canvas; 183cm x 272cm; The Rooms Provincial Art Gallery Collection. Donated by BMO Financial Group to the people of Newfoundland and Labrador in commemoration of the 60th anniversary of joining Confederation.

We can never thank the LeGrow family enough for countless acts of kindness and encouragement.

We owe much to our knitting mentors, who contributed to the accumulated knowledge that makes this book possible. We owe even more to our readers, whose kind words and handshakes give us the desire to keep on writing.

Brutus, the intrepid cat.

PHOTO CREDITS

Listed in alphabetical order and by page number.

MEET THE AUTHORS

Christine LeGrow (left)
Shirley A. Scott.

What does it take to write a saltwater knitting book?

It begins with two friends and neighbours who love their home. Christine LeGrow is a Newfoundlander through and through. Shirley Anne Scott came from away and now lives here happily, discovering new things to appreciate every day.

A deep respect for the materials and traditions of craft in Newfoundland infuses their work. It is a touchstone for both Christine and Shirley.

Technical knowledge learned from girlhood is the foundation of all saltwater knitting designs. Christine is the owner-operator of Spindrift Handknits, an established and successful business that develops her skills daily. Shirley has researched the history of knitting and published articles and patterns for years. They are never happier than when at the needles.

A shared sense of good saltwater design makes writing a pleasure. They each have buckets full of ideas but seldom need to consult. They have the same taste. It always turns out right.

The support and encouragement of family, friends, Boulder Books, and delightful readers everywhere make it all such an adventure!

christinelegrow@nl.rogers.com

shirlthepurl@hotmail.com

SALTWATER KNITTERS

Where we live the sea is a commanding presence and a hard master. It is not often a playground. Smooth sands in tropical colours are rare here. Our sands can be as dark and mysterious as on any volcanic island. Even when the ocean wears its friendly face in the shimmering days of summer, we are wary. We can never forget the lives it has taken. Beaten by winds and hurled about by storms, our ocean is more often a cold, dark, impenetrable blue.

Saltwater knitters knit their way through all the storms of life. Whether sensing exhilarating freshness or a tinge of fear, we are twinned with the ocean. Our needles purr rhythmically, like the sound of waves. Our designs are full of the spirit of the sea, just the right thing to wear in this world of wonders that is Newfoundland.

Early knitters here spent patient years at the needles, developing practical styles that kept their families warm in this new land of cold. Their knowledge and spirit are distilled in the pages of this book. Welcome to the joys of knitting, saltwater-style.

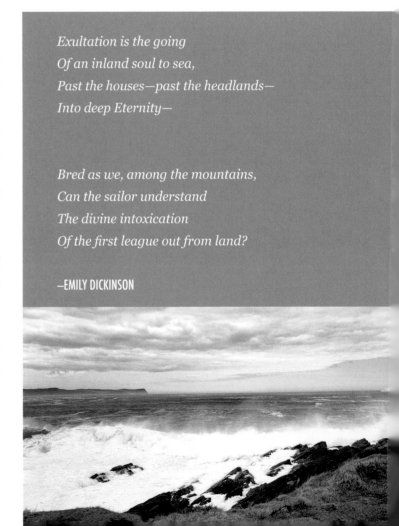

Exultation is the going
Of an inland soul to sea,
Past the houses—past the headlands—
Into deep Eternity—

Bred as we, among the mountains,
Can the sailor understand
The divine intoxication
Of the first league out from land?

—EMILY DICKINSON